The Friendship with God Collection

100 Days with Christian Mystics

MISSIONS

Uniting with God's Heart for His Lost World

Compiled and Edited
by

Bryan L. Herde

Published April 2020

Sovereign Grip Communications

Copyright© 2020 Sovereign Grip Communications

www.sovereigngrip.com

All the ends of the earth shall remember and turn to the Lord, and all the families of the nations shall worship before You. For kingship belongs to the Lord, and He rules over the nations. All the prosperous of the earth eat and worship; before Him shall bow all who go down to the dust, even the ones who could not keep themselves alive. Posterity shall serve Him; it shall be told of the Lord to the coming generation; they shall come and proclaim His righteousness to a people yet unborn, that He has done it.

Psalms 22:27-31

"Repentance and forgiveness of sins will be preached in Christ's name to all nations beginning at Jerusalem."

Luke 24:47

"Go therefore and make disciples of all nations, baptizing them in the name of the Father and of the Son and of the Holy Spirit, teaching them to observe all that I have commanded you. And behold, I am with you always, to the end of the age."

Matthew 28:19-20

"You will be My witnesses in Jerusalem, and in all Judea and Samaria, and to the ends of the earth."

Acts 1:8

After this I looked, and behold, a great multitude that no one could number, from every nation, from all tribes and peoples and languages, standing before the throne and before the Lamb, clothed in white robes, with palm branches in their hands, and crying out with a loud voice, "Salvation belongs to our God who sits on the throne, and to the Lamb!" And all the angels were standing around the throne and around the elders and the four living creatures, and they fell on their faces before the throne and worshiped God, saying, "Amen! Blessing and glory and wisdom and thanksgiving and honor and power and might be to our God forever and ever! Amen."

Revelation 7:9-12

If you would like to make any comments or ask any questions, please contact me at:
bryan@sovereigngrip.com

Dedication

This book is dedicated to the cross-cultural missionaries that I have known personally, and whom I deeply respect and love. All of them have been, or are even now, full-time, vocational missionaries. Whether spending a lifetime or less on a mission field, every one of them possesses that most indispensable attribute: *a missionary heart.*

My friends include:

Ray and Helen Elliott
Bruce and Karen Bell
Don and Mary Jo McCurry
Andy and Karen Stimer
Ben and Jamie Chase
Ed and Kathy Gray
Loren and Sylvia Eckhardt
Kirk and Violeta Nowery
Justin and Aimee Maier
Eric and Ela Sutton

Table of Contents

Short Biographies of the Writers

Rufus Anderson (1796-1880)
was an American minister who spent several decades organizing overseas missions. He graduated from Bowdoin College in 1818 and from Andover Theological Seminary in 1822, and was ordained as a minister in 1826. He worked at the American Board of Commissioners for Foreign Missions (ABCFM) as an assistant while studying at Andover. In 1822 he applied to go to India but was asked to remain at headquarters and was later appointed assistant secretary. In 1832 he was given total responsibility for overseas work as a Secretary of the ABCFM. In this capacity, he corresponded with missionaries from around the world. He traveled in Latin America (1819, 1823-1824), the Mediterranean and Near East (1828-1829, 1843-1844), India, Ceylon, Syria, and Turkey.
https://en.wikipedia.org/wiki/Rufus_Anderson

Mrs. William (Catherine) Booth (1829-1890)
was co-founder of The Salvation Army, along with her husband William Booth. Because of her influence in the formation of The Salvation Army she was known as the "Mother of The Salvation Army." Catherine Booth was eloquent and compelling in speech, articulate and devastatingly logical in writing. She had for over twenty years defended the right of women to preach the gospel on the same terms as men. At first, Catherine and her husband shared a ministry as traveling evangelists, but then she came into great demand as a preacher in her own right, especially among the well-to-do. A woman preacher was a rare phenomenon in a world where women had few civil rights and no place in the professions. Catherine Booth was both a woman and a fine preacher, a magnetic combination that attracted large numbers to hear her and made its own statement about the validity of women's ministry. She died of breast cancer at age 61 at Crossley House.
https://en.wikipedia.org/wiki/Catherine_Booth

Phillips Brooks (1835-1893)
was an American Episcopal clergyman and author, long the Rector of Boston's Trinity Church and briefly Bishop of Massachusetts, and particularly remembered as lyricist of the Christmas hymn, "O Little Town of Bethlehem."
https://en.wikipedia.org/wiki/Phillips_Brooks

Hubert W. Brown
I have been unable to find anything about him, other than the one book that was printed in 1901.

David James Burrell (1844-1926)
accepted the call as second Senior Minister in 1891 at Marble Collegiate Church in New York City, and oversaw the redesign of the church's interior. He was responsible for many of Marble's outreach programs, including sponsoring the Sunshine Mission in Hell's Kitchen and initiating the printed sermon booklets.
https://www.geni.com/people/Rev-Dr-David-Burrell/6000000009154723926

William Carey (1761-1834)
was a British Christian missionary, Particular Baptist minister, translator, social reformer and cultural anthropologist who founded the Serampore College and the Serampore University, the first degree-awarding university in India. He went to Calcutta (Kolkata) in 1793, but was forced to leave the British Indian territory by non-Baptist Christian missionaries. He joined the Baptist missionaries in the Danish colony of Frederiksnagar in Serampore. One of his first contributions was to start schools for impoverished children where they were taught reading, writing, accounting and Christianity. He opened the first theological university in Serampore offering divinity degrees, and campaigned to end the practice of *sati* [a widow throwing herself on her husband's funeral fire]. Carey is known as the "father of modern missions." His essay, *An Enquiry into the Obligations of Christians to Use Means for the Conversion of the Heathens*, led to the founding of the Baptist Missionary Society. The Asiatic Society commended Carey for "his eminent services in opening the stores of Indian literature to the knowledge of Europe and for his extensive acquaintance with the science, the natural history and

botany of this country and his useful contributions, in every branch." He translated the Hindu classic, the *Ramayana*, into English, and the Bible into Bengali, Oriya, Assamese, Marathi, Hindi and Sanskrit. William Carey has been called a reformer and illustrious Christian missionary.

https://en.wikipedia.org/wiki/William_Carey_(missionary)

Amy Beatrice Carmichael (1867-1951)

was a Protestant Christian missionary in India who opened an orphanage and founded a mission in Dohnavur. She served in India for 55 years without furlough and wrote many books about the missionary work there. While serving in India, Amy received a letter from a young lady who was considering life as a missionary. She asked Amy, "What is missionary life like?" Amy wrote back saying simply, "Missionary life is simply a chance to die." Nonetheless, in 1912 Queen Mary recognized the missionary's work, and helped fund a hospital at Dohnavur. By 1913, the Dohnavur Fellowship was serving 130 girls. In 1918, Dohnavur added a home for young boys, many born to the former temple prostitutes. Meanwhile, in 1916 Carmichael formed a Protestant religious order called Sisters of the Common Life. In 1931, a fall severely injured Carmichael, and she remained bedridden for much of her final two decades. However, it did not stop her from continuing her inspirational writing, for she published sixteen additional books, including *His Thoughts Said...His Father Said* (1951), *If* (1953), *Edges of His Ways* (1955) and *God's Missionary* (1957), as well as revised others she had previously published. Biographers differ on the number of her published works, which may have reached 35 or as many as six dozen, although only a few remain in print today. Carmichael died in India in 1951 at the age of 83. She asked that no stone be put over her grave at Dohnavur. Instead, the children she had cared for put a bird bath over it with the single inscription "Amma", which means "mother" in the Tamil language. Her example as a missionary inspired others (including Jim Elliot and his wife, Elisabeth Elliot) to pursue a similar vocation. Many webpages include quotes from Carmichael's works, such as, "It is a safe thing to trust Him to fulfill the desire that He creates."

https://en.wikipedia.org/wiki/Amy_Carmichael

William Owen Carver (1868-1954)
was born and reared in a Southern Baptist home in Tennessee. Carver graduated with an M.A. from Richmond College (now Richmond University) in 1891. Five years later, after serving briefly as a pastor and a college professor, he received a Th.M. and a Th.D. from Southern Baptist Theological Seminary, Louisville, Kentucky. He began teaching the New Testament there while a student and was elected to the faculty in 1896. Substituting for an ill colleague, Carver conducted a class in missions in 1897, and two years later he initiated a course in comparative religions and missions. He became head of the newly-founded missions department in 1900, a post he held until his retirement in 1943. He was one of the first in the United States to teach missions exclusively. Though his firsthand experience in other lands was limited to extended visits, he became a recognized authority in his field. A prolific writer, he published twenty-one books.
http://www.bu.edu/missiology/missionary-biography/c-d/carver-william-owen-1868-1954/

Robert Needham Cust (1821-1909)
was a British administrator and judge in colonial India apart from being an Anglican evangelist and linguist. He was part of the Orientalism movement and active within the British and Foreign Bible Society. He was a prolific writer and wrote on a range of subjects.
https://en.wikipedia.org/wiki/Robert_Needham_Cust

Henry Drummond (1851-1897)
was a Scottish evangelist, writer and lecturer. Drummond was born in Stirling and educated at Edinburgh University, where he displayed a strong inclination for physical and mathematical science. The religious element was an even more powerful factor in his nature, and disposed him to enter the Free Church of Scotland. While preparing for the ministry, he became for a time deeply interested in the evangelizing mission of [D. L.] Moody and [Ira] Sankey, in which he actively cooperated for two years. In 1877 he became a lecturer on natural science in the Free Church College, which enabled him to combine all the pursuits for which he felt a vocation.
https://en.wikipedia.org/wiki/Henry_Drummond_(evangelist)

Adoniram Judson (A. J.) Gordon (1836–1895)

was an American Baptist preacher, writer, composer, and founder of Gordon College and Gordon–Conwell Theological Seminary. Gordon edited two hymn books and wrote the hymn tunes for at least fifteen hymns, including "My Jesus, I Love Thee," a hymn that has been included in nearly every evangelical hymnal published from 1876 to the present time. In his book, *The Ministry of the Holy Spirit*, Gordon wrote, "It seems clear from the Scriptures that it is still the duty and privilege of believers to receive the Holy Spirit by a conscious, definite act of appropriating faith, just as they received Jesus Christ." One of his most often-quoted sayings still is, "You can do more than pray after you have prayed, but you cannot do more than pray until you have prayed."
https://en.wikipedia.org/wiki/Adoniram_Judson_Gordon

Major-General Charles George Gordon (1833-1885)

also known as "Chinese Gordon," "Gordon Pasha," and "Gordon of Khartoum," was a British Army officer and administrator. He saw action in the Crimean War as an officer in the British Army. However, he made his military reputation in China, where he was placed in command of the "Ever Victorious Army," a force of Chinese soldiers led by European officers. In the early 1860s, Gordon and his men were instrumental in putting down the Taiping Rebellion, regularly defeating much larger forces. For these accomplishments, he was given the nickname "Chinese Gordon" and honors from both the Emperor of China and the British. He entered the service of the Khedive of Egypt in 1873 (with British government approval) and later became the Governor-General of the Sudan, where he did much to suppress revolts and the local slave trade. Exhausted, he resigned and returned to Europe in 1880. A serious revolt then broke out in the Sudan, led by a Muslim religious leader and self-proclaimed Mahdi [spiritual and temporal leader] Muhammad Ahmad. In early 1884 Gordon was sent to Khartoum with instructions to secure the evacuation of loyal soldiers and civilians and to depart with them. In defiance of those instructions, after evacuating about 2,500 British civilians he retained a smaller group of soldiers and non-military men. In the buildup to battle, the two leaders corresponded, each attempting to convert the other to

his faith, but neither would accede. Besieged by the Mahdi's forces, Gordon organized a citywide defense lasting almost a year that gained him the admiration of the British public, but not of the government, which had wished him not to become entrenched. Only when public pressure to act had become irresistible did the government, with reluctance, send a relief force. It arrived two days after the city had fallen and Gordon had been killed.
https://en.wikipedia.org/wiki/Charles_George_Gordon

Samuel Dickey (S.D.) Gordon (1859-1936)

was a prolific author and evangelical minister active in the latter part of the nineteenth and early twentieth centuries. Born in Philadelphia, he served as assistant secretary of the Philadelphia Young Men's Christian Association (YMCA) in 1884-86 and then became state secretary for the YMCA in Ohio, serving from 1886 to 1895. He is perhaps best known for his series of books, *Quiet Talks About...*, which have their own unique style, very much different from that of other writers of the day.
https://en.wikipedia.org/wiki/Samuel_Dickey_Gordon

Bryan L. Herde (1955-)

was born in Enid, Oklahoma where he accepted Christ as his Savior at the age of five. Throughout his childhood and young adult years, his church was his second home. His journey with the Lord over the past decades has been one where duty has been transformed into a life of intimacy with God and whole-hearted trust in the Lord. He is happily married to his wife of 40+ years, Gayle. Bryan is a full-time business management consultant, strategic and succession planner, executive coach and part-time writer and Bible teacher. Beyond the U.S., his business and ministry travels have taken him to Libya, South Sudan, Kenya, Thailand, Haiti, Peru and Belize.

M. S. Hutton

I have been unable to find anything about him, other than the one message that was printed in 1853.

John Henry Jowett (1863-1923)

was an influential British Protestant preacher at the turn of the

nineteenth to the twentieth century and wrote many books on topics related to Christian living. Jowett was born in Beaumont Town, Northowram in Halifax, West Yorkshire to working-class parents who attended the Congregational church in Halifax, West Yorkshire. Jowett's father was a tailor and draper. Jowett understood the problems faced by workers and while pastor at Carr's Lane Congregational Church in Birmingham, England, founded the Digbeth Institute, now an arts center. Jowett was the author of numerous books on Christian devotion, preaching and the Bible.
https://en.wikipedia.org/wiki/John_Henry_Jowett

Mrs. Adoniram (Ann Hasseltine) Judson (1789-1826) was one of the first female American foreign missionaries. She married Adoniram in 1812, and two weeks later they embarked on their mission trip to India. The following year, they moved on to Burma. She had three pregnancies. The first ended in a miscarriage while moving from India to Burma; their son Roger was born in 1815 and died at eight months of age; and their third child, Maria, lived for only six months after Ann's death. While in Burma, the couple's first undertaking was to acquire the language of the locals. Missionary efforts followed, with the first local converting to Christianity in 1819. Due to liver problems, Ann returned to the United States briefly in 1822–23. During the first Anglo-Burmese war (1824–26), her husband was imprisoned for 17 months under suspicion of being an English spy, and Ann moved into a shack outside the prison gates so as to support her husband. She lobbied vigorously for months to convince the authorities to release her husband and his fellow prisoners, but her efforts were unsuccessful. She also sent food and sleeping mats to the prisoners to help their time in prison to be more bearable. During this time, Ann wrote stories of life on the mission field and the struggles she faced. She wrote tragic descriptions of child marriages, female infanticide, and the trials of the Burmese women who had no rights except for the ones their husbands gave them. Ann's health was fragile by the time her husband was released. Her efforts to be near him when he was moved to a new location, all while she was nursing a newborn child, had involved strenuous travel and living conditions that may have contributed to her illness. After her husband's release they both

remained in Burma to continue their work. Ann died at Amherst, Lower Burma, of smallpox in 1826. She wrote a catechism in Burmese, and translated the books of Daniel and Jonah into Burmese. She was the first Protestant to translate any of the scriptures into Thai when in 1819 she translated the Gospel of Matthew. Her letters home were published in periodicals such as *The American Baptist Magazine* and republished after her death as devotional writings, making both her and Adoniram celebrities in America. Her work and writings made "the role of missionary wife as a 'calling'" legitimatized for nineteenth-century Americans.
https://en.wikipedia.org/wiki/Ann_Hasseltine_Judson

Ernest A. (E.A.) Kilbourne (1865–1928)
was a missionary evangelist to Japan, Korea and China. He is best known for being a co-founder of the Oriental Missionary Society (now One Mission Society; formerly OMS International). Although Kilbourne was a quiet man, he was passionate in his writing. A friend, Paul E. Haines, recalled that Ernest's "pen frequently seared deeply into the soul consciousness of many a faulty reaper, causing them to rise, shake the dust of indifference from their sluggish feet and hasten to the battlefront, an aroused soldier of the cross." His words were powerful and effective, leading the evangelist and educator, H.C. Morrison, to say, "The writings of Ernest Kilbourne have stirred my soul more than any writings next to the Bible itself."
https://en.wikipedia.org/wiki/Ernest_A._Kilbourne

Henry Martyn (1781-1812)
was an Anglican priest and missionary to the peoples of India and Persia. Born in Truro, Cornwall, he was educated at Truro Grammar School and St John's College, Cambridge. A chance encounter with Charles Simeon led him to become a missionary. He was ordained a priest in the Church of England and became a chaplain for the British East India Company. Martyn arrived in India in April 1806, where he preached and occupied himself in the study of linguistics. He translated the whole of the New Testament into Urdu, Persian and Judaeo-Persic. He also translated the Psalms into Persian and the Book of Common Prayer into Urdu. From India, he set out for Bushire, Shiraz, Isfahan, and Tabriz [Iran]. Martyn was seized with

fever, and, though the plague was raging at Tokat, he was forced to stop there, unable to continue. On October 16, 1812 he died. He was remembered for his courage, selflessness and his religious devotion.
https://en.wikipedia.org/wiki/Henry_Martyn

George Matheson (1842-1906)
was a Scottish minister and hymn writer. He was the eldest of eight children. Matheson was educated at Glasgow Academy and the University of Glasgow, where he graduated first in classics, logic and philosophy. In his twentieth year he became totally blind, but he held to his resolve to enter the ministry, and gave himself to theological and historical study. In 1886, he moved to Edinburgh, where he became minister of St. Bernard's Parish Church in Stockbridge for 13 years. Here his chief work as a preacher was done. He died suddenly of apoplexy (stroke) at Avenell House in North Berwick on August 28, 1906 in Edinburgh.
https://en.wikipedia.org/wiki/George_Matheson

George H. Morrison (1866-1928)
was the son of a minister, born in Glasgow, Scotland. He went to the University of Glasgow in 1883 and then was offered an assistant editorship under Sir James Murray, on the staff of the New English Dictionary at Oxford. After fifteen months in Oxford he returned to Glasgow for his Divinity course. In 1893 Morrison became assistant to Alexander Whyte and the fifteen months with Whyte at St. George's, Edinburgh, altered his whole life. From 1898 to 1902 he was minister of St. John's, Dundee, a large city church. Morrison began his ministry at Wellington Church, Glasgow, on May 13, 1902, and remained there until his death in 1928.
https://www.preaching.com/articles/past-masters/george-herbert-morrison-preaching-with-clarity-and-conviction/

Andrew Murray (1828-1917)
was a South African writer, teacher and Christian pastor. Murray considered missions to be "the chief end of the church." Through his writings, Murray was also a key Higher Life or Keswick leader, and his theology of faith-healing and belief in the continuation of

the apostolic gifts made him a significant forerunner of the Pentecostal movement.

https://en.wikipedia.org/wiki/Andrew_Murray_(minister)

Joseph Parker (1830-1902)

was an English Congregational minister. Born in Hexham, Northumberland, Parker was the son of Teasdale Parker, a stonemason, and Elizabeth (née Dodd). He managed to pick up a fair education, which he constantly supplemented thereafter. Parker's preaching differed widely from his contemporaries like Spurgeon and Alexander Maclaren. He did not follow outlines or list his points, but spoke extemporaneously, inspired by his view of the spirit and attitude behind his Scripture text. He expressed himself frankly, with conviction and passion. His transcriber commented that he was at his best when he strayed furthest from his loose outlines. He did not often delve into detailed textual or critical debates. His preaching was neither systematic theology nor expository commentary, but sounded more like his personal meditations. Joseph Parker's chief legacy is not his theology but his gift for oratory. Alexander Whyte commented on Joseph Parker: "He is by far the ablest man now standing in the English-speaking pulpit. He stands in the pulpit of Thomas Goodwin, the Atlas of Independency. And Dr. Parker is a true and worthy successor to this great Apostolic Puritan." Among his biographers, Margaret Bywater called him "the most outstanding preacher of his time," and Angus Watson wrote that "no one had ever spoken like him."

https://en.wikipedia.org/wiki/Joseph_Parker_(theologian)

Arthur Tappan Pierson (1837–1911)

was an American Baptist pastor, Christian leader, missionary and writer who preached over 13,000 sermons, wrote over fifty books, and gave Bible lectures as part of a transatlantic preaching ministry that made him famous in Scotland, England, and Korea. He was a consulting editor for the original Scofield Reference Bible (1909) for his friend, C. I. Scofield and was also a friend of D. L. Moody, George Müller (whose biography, *George Muller of Bristol*, he wrote), Adoniram Judson Gordon, and C. H. Spurgeon, whom he succeeded in the pulpit of the Metropolitan Tabernacle, London,

from 1891 to 1893. Throughout his career, Pierson filled several pulpit positions around the world as an urban pastor who cared passionately for the poor. Pierson was also a pioneer advocate of faith missions who was determined to see the world evangelized in his generation. Prior to 1870, there had been only about 2000 missionaries from the United States in full-time service, roughly ten percent of whom had engaged in work among Native Americans. A great movement of foreign missions began in the 1880s and accelerated into the 20th century, in some measure due to the work of Pierson. He acted as the elder statesman of the student missionary movement and was the leading evangelical advocate of foreign missions in the late 19th century. After retiring, he visited Korea in 1910. His visiting established the Pierson Memorial Union Bible Institute (today Pyeongtaek University) in 1912.
https://en.m.wikipedia.org/wiki/Arthur_Tappan_Pierson

Albert Benjamin (A.B.) Simpson (1843-1919)

was a Canadian preacher, theologian, author, and founder of the Christian and Missionary Alliance (C&MA), an evangelical Protestant denomination with an emphasis on global evangelism. Simpson's disciplined upbringing and his natural genius made him a most effective communicator of the Word of God. His preaching brought great blessing and converts wherever he preached. Simpson composed the lyrics of over 120 hymns.
https://en.wikipedia.org/wiki/Albert_Benjamin_Simpson

Mary Mitchell Slessor (1848-1915)

was a Scottish Presbyterian missionary to Nigeria. Once in Nigeria, Slessor learned Efik, the local language, then began teaching. Because of her understanding of the native language and her bold personality, Slessor gained the trust and acceptance of the locals and was able to spread Christianity while promoting women's rights and protecting native children. She is most famous for having stopped the common practice of infanticide of twins among the Ibibio people, an ethnic group in southeastern Nigeria.
https://en.wikipedia.org/wiki/Mary_Slessor

Eli Smith (1801-1857)

was an American Protestant Missionary and scholar, born at

Northford, Connecticut. He graduated from Yale in 1821 and from Andover Theological Seminary in 1826. He is known for bringing the first printing press with Arabic type to Syria. He went on to pursue the task which he considered to be his life's work: translation of the Bible into Arabic.
https://en.wikipedia.org/wiki/Eli_Smith

Francis Wayland (1796-1865)

was an American Baptist educator and economist. Wayland was born in New York City, New York. He was president of Brown University and pastor of the First Baptist Church in America in Providence, Rhode Island. In Washington, D.C., Wayland Seminary was established in 1867, primarily to educate former slaves, and was named in his honor. In 1899, Wayland Seminary merged with another school to become the current Virginia Union University at Richmond, Virginia.
https://en.wikipedia.org/wiki/Francis_Wayland

Maria A. West (1800's, specific years not known)

was an American missionary to Turkey and worked primarily with the Armenian populace. She went there in 1852. The book she wrote, *The Romance of Missions*, from which her contributions were drawn, provided a dynamic perspective of a wide-ranging work among the Armenian peoples, mostly women and children, located in Turkey. She was a teacher who worked in a number of towns and villages throughout her career.

Drawn from her book, *The Romance of Missions*, published by Anson D. F. Randolph & Company, New York, in 1875

Matthew Tyson Yates (1819-1888)

was a Baptist Christian missionary who served with the American Southern Baptist Mission during the late Qing Dynasty in China. Matthew and Eliza Yates opened Southern Baptist missionary work in Shanghai, China, in 1847 and continued working there for over forty years until their deaths. Matthew was born into a farmer's home near Raleigh, North Carolina. He was one of ten children. His parents were strong Christians who were active leaders in their local Baptist church. He trusted Christ as his Savior through the encouragement of a traveling pastor who urged him to pray, "Lord, be merciful to me, a sinner." Almost immediately upon his conversion, he began to pray a second prayer, "Lord, what will you have me do?" Matthew was made aware of the overwhelming lostness of the world after he read the life story of missionary Ann Judson. He wrote that after reading her biography, he would weep for hours while plowing the fields as he reflected on the condition of those who "knew nothing of Jesus Christ, the only Savior of the world." Despite illness, loneliness, and opposition, Yates continued to serve for forty-one years until his death. On March 19, 1888, as his body was being taken from his house for burial, one thousand copies of his translation of the New Testament (minus Revelation) were delivered to the front door of the Shanghai Baptist church.

Drawn from *The Story of Yates the Missionary*, by Charles E. Taylor, published by Sunday School Board, Southern Baptist Convention, Nashville, TN in 1898

Samuel M. Zwemer (1867-1952)

was nicknamed the "Apostle to Islam" and was an American missionary, traveler, and scholar. He was born at Vriesland, Michigan. After being ordained to the Reformed Church ministry in 1890, he was a missionary at Busrah, Bahrein, and at other locations in Arabia from 1891 to 1905. He was a member of the Arabian Mission (1890–1913). Zwemer served in Egypt from 1913 to 1929. He also traveled widely in Asia Minor, and was elected a fellow of the Royal Geographical Society of London. In 1929 he was appointed professor of missions and professor of the history of religion at Princeton Theological Seminary, where he taught until 1937. He was famously turned down by the American Missionary Society, which resulted in him going overseas alone. He founded and edited the publication *The Moslem World* for thirty-five years. He was influential in mobilizing many Christians to go into missionary work in Islamic countries.

https://en.wikipedia.org/wiki/Samuel_Marinus_Zwemer

Introduction

"Take off your sandals, for the place where you are
standing is holy ground."
Exodus 3:5

Walking on the ground where martyrs died. Visiting the grave of a missionary who had passed into glory a long time ago. Watching a pastor unable to talk about the horrors he has witnessed. And personally moved to tears and speechlessness. These were holy moments, profound feelings, being on holy ground. All happened during three days in South Sudan in 2008.

As I have worked to put together this collection, the words God spoke to Moses in the wilderness resonated deeply in me. Not only because of my own experience in South Sudan, but because I see that God—from the very beginning in the Garden of Eden—has been the One who pursues lost men and women over time and throughout the world. His heart is the one that is restless, anxious and stirred deeply to do whatever is needed to save as many as would believe.

God's heart is a "missionary heart." And any person whose heart has been melded into oneness with His will possess a missionary heart as well. A "missionary heart" is a heart that is in sync with God's. A heart that is so surrendered to Him that He is completely free to work in, through and with each individual according to His own desires, plans and will. For each of us, that will mean transformation into a person whose all is controlled by the Holy Spirit. Once one's will is yielded to the control of the Holy Spirit, the King Himself will take all responsibility for choosing where you reside, what you do, and when you do it.

As you will gather from the material within this book, your participation in missions really is determined by your personal synchronization with God's heart. Whether through prayer, giving, short-term trips or even a move to a foreign country, missions is a decision of the heart, and "where your treasure is, there your heart will be also" (Matthew 6:21).

Having a missionary heart is the first call for every believer, every child of God, every disciple of Christ. Throughout the enclosed sermons, letters and reports you will hear the appeal to be fully yielded to the Lord in order for Him to have complete control of you. Then whatever He chooses thereafter He will make plain to you in His time, for His purposes and for His glory.

> Jesus is the Chief Executive of the campaign through His Spirit. The direction of it belongs to Him. He knows best what each one can do. He knows best what needs to be done. He is ambitious that each of us shall be the best and have the best. He has a plan thought out for each life and for the whole campaign. His Spirit is in us to administer His plan. He never sleeps. He gives to every person specifically as He will. And His is a loving, wise will. It can be trusted.
>
> Samuel Dickey (S. D.) Gordon

In 2008, I visited Sudan. This was after the end of their most recent civil war and prior to the division into Sudan and South Sudan. One day we went to visit the site of the construction of a new church building in Kajo Keji, made necessary by the mass burnings of churches by the attacking forces, oftentimes while still occupied. The pastor was holding his toddler and talking to us. When asked to tell a bit about his time over the past 25 years while on the run from the Islamic Northern Sudanese military, he had a faraway look in his eyes. He was completely unable to speak. But one could see that his mind had gone back to memories too horrible to describe.

Another day we attended a church service in Yei. It was a marvelous time of worship with Sudanese Christians praising God and celebrating their newly-built church, replacing yet another one destroyed by the hostile army. The people had just returned from their own time as refugees. After the service, we were taken to visit the neglected grave site of one of the original missionaries to the area. It was a somber, yet joyful, moment.

During the war and resulting genocide, more than two million civilians were killed. And many of those were Christians. As I walked on the ground in three parts of that country, I knew I was walking where many, many men, women and children had died, where thousands had fled for their lives, and where now, by God's grace, His Church still lives and His glorious name is still praised. I was deeply humbled and changed for life.

But I also learned that the saving work of Jesus Christ—as lived and proclaimed by missionaries from decades before I was there—had instilled in the people an anchor of truth and a hope that would not die. And no barbarous and ruthless efforts by spiritual and physical enemies could extinguish the truth and the power of Christ in and through His Church. Those memories have been refreshed by the work invested in this anthology of beautiful, powerful and relevant messages as delivered by brothers and sisters in Christ over one hundred to two hundred years ago. In that context, I have chosen to compile this collection of missions-oriented sermons and letters to make you aware of some very important truths:

- The nineteenth century was when the Church was mobilized to launch into global missions at an unprecedented scale.

- Men and women were moved by the Holy Spirit in relatively large numbers to literally "go and die" on a foreign field of God's choosing. Once they left home, it was expected that they would never return.

- Sermons about the call to be a missionary, to be involved in missions in the churches, to pray for missions and all that included, and to give generously were far more common than are heard in our churches today.

- Many of the sermons and letters inside this book include stories about what God was doing around the world at that time. Additionally, as the world was being discovered, an understanding of other religions, cultures and opportunities led to an awakening as to how the rest of the world lived.

- The fire, the zeal and the truths contained in these sermons and letters are timeless, powerful and convicting for every one of us who takes the time to read them.

- The spiritual decline of western Europe's churches, and those in America, has meant that foreign missions have taken a back seat to numerous other issues being embraced by today's churches.

It is my hope and prayer that through these sermons you will be profoundly moved and will synchronize with the beating of God's heart in a fresh way, and that you will, as a result, give Him your all to do with as He pleases. If you have already surrendered your heart and life to the Lord, then be encouraged and moved to new a commitment to what the Lord wants to do through His Church and for His Kingdom throughout the world.

> Self is too small an object for the vast active powers with which our Maker has given us. They can be fully expended upon nothing less than the great work He has made us for and assigned us. Give yourselves wholly to this work, though it is by still laboring upon your farm or at your place of business, and then will you find that for the first time you are in your proper place. You are doing just what God intended you should do, and the soul is satisfied.
>
> Eli Smith

Editor's Notes

All of the sermons within are taken from books and pamphlets published before 1923. Consequently, are all "public domain" materials.

I continue to be extremely grateful to **www.archive.org** for the vast resources they are still building by converting millions of out-of-print books (and more) into PDFs that are made available to the public free of charge. Thank you!

Mystics

When using the term "Christian mystics," I will, of course offend some and confuse others. But I am in good company. A. W. Tozer (prominent American pastor, 1897-1963) had the same difficulty. Tozer explains that a "mystic" is one who partakes in the "personal spiritual experience" that saints of Biblical and post-Biblical times enjoyed. He is speaking of "the evangelical mystic who has been brought by the gospel into intimate fellowship with the Godhead."

So how does the mystic differ from other Christians? Tozer answers:

> The mystic experiences his faith down in the depths of his sentiment being while the other does not. He exists in a world of spiritual reality. He is quietly, deeply, and sometimes almost ecstatically aware of the Presence of God in his own nature and in the world around him. His religious experience is sometimes elemental, as old as time and the creation. It is immediate acquaintance with God by union with the Eternal Son. It is to know that which passes knowledge.

I am certainly not in perfect agreement with all of the various positions that the many authors in this book held on every Christian doctrine, philosophy or experience. However, the Christian mystics I have selected meet that most basic quality that was true of each of them: they burned with a passion for a deep, intimate, unfiltered and unfettered relationship with God—a synchronizing of hearts and minds with His. God's grace and love cover a multitude of sins!

One further note of explanation about Christian mystics from Tozer:

> Back on the farm in Pennsylvania, we had an old apple tree. It was a gnarly, stark-looking tree. A casual glance at this tree might tempt a person to pass it up. Regardless of how terrible the tree looked, however, it produced some of the most delicious apples I have ever eaten. I endured the gnarly branches in order to enjoy the delicious fruit. I feel the same way about some of these grand old mystics of the Church. They may look gnarly and austere, but they produced wonderful spiritual fruit. The fruit is what really matters, not the appearance. It matters not if the man wears a robe or a suit; it is the man that really counts. I am willing to overlook a lot if the writer genuinely knows God and "knows God other than by hearsay," as Thomas Carlyle used to say. Too many only repeat what they have heard from somebody who heard it from somebody else. It is refreshing to hear an original voice. Each of these mystics had that original voice.

Tozer's comments are excerpted from
https://immoderate.wordpress.com/2006/01/26/a-w-tozer-on-the-christian-mystic-2/

Editing

I have taken the liberty to do some content editing in six ways. I have:

1. Deleted some portions that did not contribute to the theme of this book. These are noted by "***" or "…".

2. Exchanged archaic or difficult words with more modern synonyms.

3. Updated "King James" English into more modern terms, such as "thee," and "ye" to "you"; and most words ending in "eth" such as "abideth" and "trusteth" into "abides" and "trusts," etc.

4. Capitalized all pronouns (hopefully) that refer to God, Jesus and the Holy Spirit. I have done this for two reasons: the first is that I love the reverence for God that it demonstrates; and, secondly, it helps ensure clarity as to precisely who is being discussed.

5. Reworked some phrases or sentences that were just hard to understand into what I trust keeps the intent of the original.

6. Where possible, I have changed the general use of the male words "men," "mankind," and "men." Up until the latter part of the 20th century, the male term was universally understood to refer to all people. For the most part, no one who is teaching in this book ever intended purposefully to exclude women or even children from the applications of these truths. In fact, there are numerous stories in this book of many women missionaries whom God used throughout this time period in profound and significant ways.

However, you will quickly notice that I did not go so far as to change any of the messages completely into twenty-first-century English. They are still, in both tone and voice, true to their age.

Attitudes

You may perceive some apparent "superiority" or "paternalism" in the attitudes or views among the missionaries concerning the people whom they encountered in their fields of service. It is impossible for us now, one to two hundred years later, to really comprehend the shock and even horror they felt when they encountered native practices such as cannibalism, infanticide (especially regarding twins and female babies), wives dying in the cremation fires of their husbands (*sati*), witchcraft, demonic possession, as well as diseases, hunger, wars, illiteracy (due to unwritten languages) and much, much more. Added to these are the disregard and diminishment of women who were treated as property, or even as animals by their husbands. What missionaries brought to the cultures of so many peoples, in addition to the gospel, were changes in education, humanitarianism, healthcare, nutrition and many other benefits.

Terms

On the next two pages, I have tried to define some terms that you will encounter frequently:

> **Providence/providential**: This refers to God's sovereignty, God's working, God's involvement, God's control. It was a commonly-used term prior to the twentieth century. This grand word appears very often throughout many of the writings within this book.

> **Holiness Movement/Associations**: This was a controversial movement in the 1800's that found many adherents, as well as many opponents. Holiness groups tended to oppose antinomianism, which is a theological framework that states that God's law is done away with. Holiness groups believe the moral aspects of the law of God were pertinent for the day, inasmuch as the law was completed in Christ. This position attracted opposition from some evangelicals, who charged that such an attitude refutes or slights Reformation teachings, particularly Calvinism, that believers are justified by grace through faith and not through any efforts or states of mind on their part, and that the effects of original sin remain even in the most faithful of souls. From what I gather from some of the writings included (and not included) in this book, those who opposed this movement seemed to feel that the emphasis upon personal experience eclipsed vital engagement in missionary activities. According to a couple of the writers in this book,

the proponents of holiness were too inwardly focused and not enough outwardly concerned.

Pentecostal: When this term is used throughout this book, it is referring back to the Day of Pentecost, not to the charismatic movement and/or denominations of churches that exist today. It is used as an adjective for what churches should be, regarding the power of the Holy Spirit working freely.

"Church" or "church": When the capitalized word, "Church" is used, it refers to the universal body of Christ— the overall body of born-again believers. The small "church" is used when referring to a local gathering, or a group of specified gatherings.

Heathen/heathenism/heathendom: A broad term used to describe all those who are not aware of or believe in the gospel of Jesus Christ and subsequently, receive Him as their personal Savior.

Gospel: The "Good News" of Jesus Christ, as clearly expressed in the Gospel of John, chapter three, verses 16-18 (NIV): "For God so loved the world that He gave His one and only Son, that whoever believes in Him shall not perish but have eternal life. For God did not send His Son into the world to condemn the world, but to save the world through Him. Whoever believes in Him is not condemned, but whoever does not believe stands condemned already because they have not believed in the name of God's one and only Son."

Civilized: This refers to the development of a written language, educational systems, removal of violent and abhorrent practices such as cannibalism, mass murders of people when royalty dies, among many other notable changes and refinements.

Prayer Closet: This is derived from the King James Version of Matthew 6:6, "But thou, when thou prayest, enter into thy closet, and when thou hast shut thy door, pray to thy Father which is in secret…" It is a term frequently used for simply going to spend some private, quiet time talking with God.

Powerful Quotes Concerning Missions

Missions are the chief end of the Church. All the work of the Holy Spirit in converting sinners and sanctifying believers has this for its one aim—to equip them for the part that each must at once take in winning back the world to God. Nothing less than what God's eternal purpose and Christ's dying love aimed at can be the aim of the Church.
Andrew Murray

The dry rot of modern Christianity is selfishness, worldliness and love of ease, the pursuit of pleasure, the gratification of our own desires. All this is incompatible with true love to Christ, but all this the heart will cling to until it is lifted out of it by a superior passion. This cannot be accomplished by the conventional type of religious life. A stronger force is needed: the more glorious and consuming flame of heavenly love.
Albert B. Simpson

Let me plead for the foreign missionary idea as the necessary completion of the Christian life. It is the apex to which all the lines of the pyramid lead up. The Christian life without it is a mangled and imperfect thing. The glory and the heroism of Christianity lie in its missionary life.
Phillips Brooks

The Master's say-so is accepted by Spirit-led people as final. He chooses Peter to open the door to the outer nations, and Paul to enter the opened door. He chooses not an apostle but Philip [the deacon, Acts 21:8] to open up Samaria, and Titus to guide church matters in Crete. A miner's son [Martin Luther] is chosen to shake Europe, and a cobbler [William Carey] to kindle anew the missionary fires of Christendom. [David] Livingstone is sent to open up the heart of Africa for a fresh infusion of the blood of the Son of

God. A nurse-maid, whose name remains unknown, is used to mold for God the child who became the seventh Earl of Shaftsbury [Anthony Ashley-Cooper], one of the most truly Spirit-filled people of the world. George Müller is chosen for the significant service of re-teaching people that God still lives and actually answers prayer. George Williams and Robert McBurney become the leaders, British and American, in an in-Spirited movement [YMCA] to win young men by thousands…The common factor in all is the Chooser.
Samuel Dickey (S. D.) Gordon

The man or the woman who longs to be a missionary, but whose yearnings cannot be realized, is counted as a missionary in the eyes of the Lord, and the will to do is reckoned as the deed done. "You did well that it was in your heart" [1 Kings 8:18].
John Henry Jowett

And is there in reality one set of obligations laid upon missionaries, and another more lenient set upon the rest of the community? Where will you find them prescribed? In the Bible? I do not know what page. I discover no distinction made there between missionaries and yourselves. They are not singled out by a solitary requirement that is not equally aimed at others. Where is it said to them, deny yourself, and the same broad command does not rest equally on you? The providence of God has called them indeed to go in person, as missionaries, and to you He may not have pointed out such a course. But has He thereby imposed upon them an obligation to self-denial from which you are exempted? Are you not bound to labor equally hard at home in the same great work? The type of self-denial laid on you, and the place in which it is to be practiced, are different; but does not the amount pressing upon both remain the same? I really cannot find that God has imposed upon me one obligation to make more sacrifices as a missionary than others are bound to make as Christians, however different in kind our respective sacrifices may be.
Eli Smith

The name "disciple" was often on the lips of Christ, and is familiar on the gospel page. But it is very significant that, as the days went by, and people perceived all that they owed to Christ, the name of

disciple (for all its tender memories) gave way to that of servant or slave. That indicates with what a perfect mastery Jesus Christ controls the individual. His influence reaches to the depths of being and possesses every power and every passion. Yet just as notable as that complete control is the area over which it is to reach: "Go into all the world, and preach the gospel to every creature." The two remarkable things about the gospel are that it is deep as life and wide as all the world. It is a message of redeeming power for the whole person; it is a message of redeeming power for everyone.
George H. Morrison

Every one of us, whether old or young, can play a part in this unequalled labor, and help advance—more powerfully than we know—the promised evangelization of the world. Read, I pray you, with attention the story of that service in our missionary journals; take an intelligent interest in the matter, as I know so many of you already do; give it a large place in daily prayer and do not be content with general petitions but, with a mind enriched by information, intercede for particular localities. It is in such ways that we can take our place, though we may not stand in the forefront of the battle. By prayer, by interest, by thoughtful giving, we can help the worldwide triumph of the gospel. For that great victory will surely come when the knowledge of Christ shall cover the whole earth, and happy shall be the one who, in that crowning hour, shall be found to have hastened on its coming.
George H. Morrison

The chief, Sechele, of the Bakwains in Botswana, on first hearing the gospel, was much affected and asked David Livingstone, "How is it that your forefathers did not send to my forefathers news of these things sooner?"
From *The Missionary Heroes of Africa* by J. H. Morrison, Published 1922

The Committee of the Society held a farewell meeting on April 25, 1876, and at that meeting Alexander Mackay made some very memorable remarks. Speaking last he said, "There is one thing which my brethren have not said, and which I wish to say. I want to remind the Committee that within six months they will probably

hear that one of us is dead." These words, spoken by a slim, blue-eyed boy, were startling, and there was a silence in the room that might be felt. Then he went on, "Yes, is it at all likely that eight Englishmen should start for Central Africa and all be alive six months after? One of us at least—it may be I—will surely fall before that." "But," he added, "what I want to say is this: When that news comes, do not be cast down, but send someone else immediately to take the vacant place."
From *The Missionary Heroes of Africa* by J. H. Morrison

The death of Christ supplies the motive of missionary enterprise. When love is nothing and moral law is everything, you have a period when not a hand is lifted for the salvation of the heathen world. For it is not morality that seeks the world: it is religion centering in love. It is a view of a divine love so wonderful that it stooped to the service of death upon a cross. So always, in evangelical revival, when that has been understood in the wonder of it, the passion to tell it has come again, and people have carried the message to mankind.
George H. Morrison

The year 1887 was memorable in the annals of the Mission as "the Black Year," when six of the missionaries died in seven months. George Grenfell was at home on furlough, but on hearing of the first four deaths he hastened his return to the field, although his health was precarious. On reaching the Congo he was met with the news of two more deaths. Friends of the Mission at home were stunned by these losses, and spoke of withdrawing from so deadly a field. But Grenfell was resolute. "We can't continue as we are," he wrote. "It is either advance or retreat. But if you retreat, you must not count on me. I will be no party to it, and you will have to do without me. I might plead with the Churches that for the sake of our great Head, for the sake of the terrible sin-stricken 'heart of Africa,' that out of love for and regard to the memory of our dear Comber, who died just a year ago, that for each and all of these reasons they should keep their pledges, but my heart is hot within me, and I feel I cannot plead. If love and duty and sacred promises are nothing, nothing that I can say will avail."
From *The Missionary Heroes of Africa* by J. H. Morrison

"I, Maung Nau, the constant recipient of your excellent favor, approach your feet. Whereas my lords three have come to the country of Burma, not for the purpose of trade, but to preach the religion of Jesus Christ, the Son of the eternal God, I, having heard and understood, am, with a joyful mind, filled with love. I believe that the Divine Son, Jesus Christ, suffered death in the place of men to atone for their sins. Like a heavy laden man, I feel my sins are very many. The punishment of my sins I deserve to suffer. Since it is so, Sirs, do consider that I, taking refuge in the merits of the Lord Jesus Christ and receiving baptism in order to become His disciple, shall dwell with yourselves, a band of brothers, in the happiness of heaven, and grant me the ordinance of baptism. It is through the grace of Christ that you, Sirs, have come by ship from one country and continent to another, and that we have met together. I pray my lords three that a suitable day may be appointed, and that I may receive the ordinance of baptism. And it is only since I have met with you, Sirs, that I have known about the eternal God. I venture to pray that you will still unfold to me the religion of God, that my old disposition may be destroyed and my new disposition improved."
Request made to Adoniram Judson by the first convert in Burma

I know what some of you are saying in your hearts whenever we talk together about foreign missions. "There are heathen here in Boston," you declare, "heathen enough here in America. Let us convert them first, before we go to China." That plea we all know, and I think it sounds more cheap and more shameful every year. What can be more shameful than to make the imperfection of our Christianity at home an excuse for not doing our work abroad? It is as shameless as it is shameful. It pleads for exemption and indulgence on the ground of its own neglect and sin. It is like a murderer of his father asking the judge to have pity on his orphan-hood. Even the people who make such a plea feel, I think, how unheroic it is. The minister who does what they bid him do feels his task of preaching to such people perhaps all the more necessary but certainly all the less heroic, as he sees how utterly they have failed to feel the very nature of the gospel which he preaches to them.
Phillips Brooks

It seems to me that the churches at home have almost forgotten Foreign Missions. No one comes to my aid. There is something wrong. When people have much of the spirit of Christ, they have the spirit of missions. It is the duty of pastors to teach their people to observe all things whatsoever Christ commanded them.
Matthew E. Yates

It is a little heroic even to believe in foreign missions. If we may not be among the heroes, let us, like the church of old, hear the Holy Ghost and go with Paul and Barnabas down to their ship and lay our hands on them and send them away with all our sympathy and blessing. So, perhaps, we can catch something of their heroism. So, in our quiet and home-keeping Christian lives, the idea of Christianity may become more clear, Christ our Lord more dear, and we ourselves be made more faithful, more generous, and more brave.
Phillips Brooks

100 Days with Christian Mystics

MISSIONS
Uniting with God's Heart for His Lost World

DAY 1
A Finishing Work: Part 1 of 2
by Ernest A. Kilbourne
(Excerpted from *The Great Commission*, published by Oriental Missionary Society, Tokyo, Japan in 1913)

The days are weighty with momentous happenings; the air seems darkened with threatening events; the world is daily startled and horrified, or rather it is becoming accustomed to startling and horrifying occurrences. There are upheavals in nature, in society, among the nations, and in religious circles today which have scarcely been equaled in all history. This is a day of trials, of testing, of sifting, a day of judgment for God's children. God is beginning to do a quick work in the earth, and woe unto the unstable and wavering ones who do not cast away their doubts and fears and launch out upon the broad bosom of full salvation! Many will be brought to learn righteousness only through the judgment fires which are in the earth today.

As one looks out upon the swiftly changing scenes of this latter day, they are indeed vividly impressed that God is working a work in all the earth that foreshadows coming events with a vengeance. We are wise if we see the hand of God. We are forewarned, we are forearmed, we are equipped to fit in with the Divine purpose. So, beloved, let us keep on our faces before Him, let our ear be swift to catch the voice in the thunders of trouble, or in the winds of trial, or in the earthquakes of affliction, or in the still small voice whispering in our innermost soul. Let us be awake and watching, alive to God's expectations for us. Let us beware of Satan's "angel of light" methods, and of his sluggish servings which would paralyze our efforts to obey all the will of God; let us be careful that he does not blind our eyes so that we are unable to see God's plan for us, and keep us groping about in the dark. How sad it is to see so many of God's children blinded by Satan so that they cannot lift up their eyes to look out upon the ripened fields of heathendom. He blinds many with multiplied labors at their own feet, he keeps many so busy with their own selfish interests that they are never forced to think of the unnumbered millions who have never heard of Jesus. O how God's heart must often be grieved by the apathy and lethargy of many of His children! Beloved...let us get a look at things from God's standpoint in our prayer closets on our knees, which will lift us once and forever out of our narrow boundaries into a wide place of usefulness, reaching out our arms to a whole world of lost sinners. Let us get such a flood of glory in our souls that our rivers will indeed...bring life to those whom Jesus has redeemed through His own precious blood.

O for a host of stalwart giants whose vision is unhindered by man-made boundaries, whose faith leaps over every human obstacle of prejudice and strides with a conqueror's pace to the ends of the earth in search of lost souls! Those whom God delights in; those whom God can trust in any kind of battle; people who God can depend on at any moment of the day for any service, be it great or small; those who will not flinch at any earthly foe, but will go all the way with God!...O beloved let us be that one! Human courage, natural force is as impotent as the spray beating against the rocks of time, but there is a courage, there is a power in Christ which is not "might" nor "strength," but is mighty through God for the pulling down of the strongholds of Satan and laying low everything that elevates itself against the knowledge of God. Beloved, that is what the baptism with the Holy Ghost and fire does for us. When we get the Holy Ghost we move out of commonplace things and get a grip on eternal things, and bring disaster to the devil's kingdom at home and abroad. The Holy Ghost is not that weak thing many are professing to have, and those who bring dishonor to God's cause by their profession. He is ever a burning fire, a flaming tongue, whether to the ignorant or to the learned. He is the same Holy Ghost who descended on the day of Pentecost.

DAY 2
A Finishing Work: Part 2 of 2
by Ernest A. Kilbourne

(Excerpted from *The Great Commission*, published by Oriental Missionary Society, Tokyo, Japan in 1913)

Beloved, let us measure ourselves in the light of what His coming is going to reveal in our own personal service. Have we been zealous to obey God's Word concerning "every creature?" Have we been anxious to go and pray? Have we given ourselves in a whole-hearted consecration to God for the "regions beyond," as well as at home? Have we obeyed God's command to "lift up our eyes and look on the fields?" Have we been passionate in spirit in our prayer closets? Have we lifted up our voices against the indifference and lethargy of people to get the gospel to the ends of the earth? Have we stayed long enough on our knees to hear from God concerning these things, or have we been afraid of the voice of God, and hurried from our prayer closets in case He should tell us something we dreaded to hear?

As a pastor, have you been intimidated from preaching that missionary sermon because you feared that the people might forget your own personal needs, and give all their money for missions instead of to you? If so, such money must curse rather than bless, for it is blood money, won at the cost of perishing souls. Has the devil been shaking the empty bread-basket in your face, and telling you that if you preach on missions, your wife and children will starve? Well, they would starve in a good cause and be crowned in glory. Some have starved on the mission field, but we have yet to hear of anyone starving because they gave their all to support the missionary. Never fear, beloved, God will not let such people starve, He needs them too badly. When they give all their tithes He pours out stores of blessing so they can give more.

"I beseech you therefore, brethren, by the mercies of God that you present your bodies a living sacrifice" to come, to pray, or to give, so that you may have confidence and boldness in the day of His coming, and not be ashamed before Him; but, knowing that you have done what you could, there is no cause for regret, no condemnation, no finger of reproach from any unsaved heathen of any nation.

Let us so measure up that our lives will be a continual reprimand to those who are asleep on this question of evangelizing a lost world. Let us so serve Him in fervency of spirit that our zeal will kindle other hearts, and the missionary spirit will spread like the fire of Samson's foxes, and burn up the selfish indulgences which hinder the children of God from getting the "glad tidings of great joy" published in every nation and to "every creature." Amen!

DAY 3
The World's Need: Part 1 of 2
by Catherine Booth
(Excerpted from *Papers on Aggressive Christianity*, published by The Salvation Army, London, England in 1891)

"Son, go and work in the vineyard."
Matthew 21:28

"And the master said to the servant, 'Go out to the highways and hedges and compel people to come in, that my house may be filled.'"
Luke 14:23

It seems to me that no one can disinterestedly and dispassionately study the New Testament without arriving at the conclusion that it is a fundamental principle, underlying the whole, that His light and grace is expansive; that is, God has, in no case, given His light, His truth, and His grace to any individual soul without holding that soul responsible for communicating that light and grace to others. Real Christianity is, in its very nature and essence, aggressive. We get this principle fully exhibited and illustrated in the parables of Jesus Christ. If you will study them you will find that He has not given us anything to be used merely for ourselves, but that we hold and possess every talent which He has committed to us for the good of others, and for the salvation of others. If I understand it, I say this is a fundamental principle of the New Testament.

How wonderfully this principle was exhibited in the lives of the apostles and early Christians! How utterly careless they seemed to be about everything compared with this—this was the first thing with them everywhere! How Paul, at the very threshold, counted nothing else of any consequence, but willingly, cheerfully gave up every other consideration to live for this; and how he speaks of other apostles and helpers in the gospel who had been near unto death, and laid down their lives for the work's sake; and we know how he traveled, worked, prayed, wept, and suffered, bled and died, for this one end. And also with the early Christians, who were scattered through the persecutions, how they went everywhere preaching the Word; how earnest and zealous they were, even after the Apostolic age. We learn from church history how they would push themselves in everywhere; how they made converts, and won real, self-denying followers even in kings' courts; how they would not be kept out, and could not be put down, and could not be hindered or silenced. "These Christians are everywhere," said one of their bitterest persecutors. Yes, they were ready in season and out of season; they won men and women on every hand, to the irritation and annoyance of those who hated them. Like their Master, they could not be hidden; they could not be repressed; so aggressive, so compelling was the Spirit which inspired and urged them on.

It becomes a greater puzzle every day to me, coming in contact with individual souls, how people read their Bibles! They do not seem to understand what they read. Well might a Philip or an angel come to them and say, "Do you understand what you are reading?" Oh! friends, study your New Testament on this question, and you will be alarmed to find out to what tremendous extent you are your brother's keeper—to what a profound and alarming extent God holds you responsible for the salvation of those around you...

We are called by the Word...by the underlying principle running through it all, and laying upon us the obligation to save the lost. In fact, the world is cast upon us: we are the only people who can save the unconverted.

DAY 4
The World's Need: Part 2 of 2
by Catherine Booth
(Excerpted from *Papers on Aggressive Christianity*, published by The Salvation Army, London, England in 1891)

Matthew 21:28; Luke 14:23

Oh! I wish I could get this thought thoroughly into your minds. It has been, perhaps, one of the most potent—with respect to any little service I have rendered in the vineyard, the thought that Jesus Christ has nobody else to represent Him here but us Christians—His real people: nobody else to work for Him. These poor people of the world, who are in darkness and ignorance, have nobody else to show them the way of mercy. If we do not go to them with loving earnestness and determination to rescue them from the grasp of the great enemy; if we do not, by the power of the Holy Ghost, bind the strong man and take his goods [Satan, Matthew 12:29], who is to do it? God has delegated it to us. I say this is an alarming and monumental consideration.

We are called by the Spirit. The very first desire of a newly-born soul is seeking after some other lost soul. The very first utterance, after the first burst of praise to God for deliverance from the bondage of sin and death, is a prayer gasped to the throne for some other soul still in darkness. And is this not the legitimate fruit of the Spirit? Is this not what we should expect? I take anyone here, who has been truly saved, to record if the first outpourings of their soul, after their own deliverance, was not for somebody else—father, mother, child, brother, sister, friend? Oh! Yes, some of you could not go to sleep until you had written to a distant relative and poured out your soul in anxious longings for his or her salvation; you could not take your necessary food until you had spoken or written to somebody in whose soul you were deeply interested. The Spirit began at once to urge you to seek for souls; and so it is frequently the last cry of the Spirit in the believer's soul before it leaves the body. You have sat beside many a dying saint, and what has been the last prayer? Has it been anything about self, money, family, circumstances? Oh! Those things are now all left behind, and the last expressed anxiety has been for some prodigal soul outside the kingdom of God.

When the light of eternity comes streaming upon the soul, and its eyes get wide open to the value of souls, it neither hears nor sees anything else! It goes out of time into eternity, praying as the Redeemer did, for the souls it is leaving behind. This is the first and last utterance of the Spirit in the believer's soul on earth; and oh! if Christians were only true to the promptings of this blessed Spirit, it would be the prevailing impulse, the first desire and effort all the way through life. It is not God's fault that it is not so. In personal dealing with souls there is no point that comes out more frequently than this: nothing which those who have really been converted and have become backsliders in heart more frequently confess and bemoan than their unfaithfulness to the warnings of the Spirit with respect to other souls. In fact, backsliding begins here in thousands of instances. Satan gets people to yield to considerations of ease, politeness, being out of season, being careless, and so on; and they lose opportunities of dealing with souls, and so the Spirit is grieved again and again. Oh! what numbers of people have confessed this to me.

The world is dying. Do you believe it? You are called by the wants of the world. Begin nearest home if you like, by all means. I have little faith in those people's service who go abroad after others, while their own are perishing at their firesides…I wish Christians would weep the gospel into people; it would often go deeper than it does…Go to the prayer closet until you get filled with the Spirit, and then go and let Him out upon them.

by George H. Morrison

(http://devotionals.ochristian.com/george-h-morrison-devotional-sermons-complete.shtml)

"And I, when I am lifted up from the earth, will draw all people to Myself."
John 12:32

The Motive of Missionary Enterprise

It is the death of Christ which supplies the motive for the missionary enterprise.

We must remember that when we speak of the death of Christ, we speak of a death different from our own. Our death is the ceasing of activity; Christ's was the crown and climax of His life. "I have power to lay it down," He said, and that is a power no other person has shared. We die when our appointed hour comes, and when the hand of God has touched us, and we sleep. But Christ never looked upon His death like that, as something inevitable and irresistible. He looked on it as the last free glorious service of a life that had always been a life of love. Here in one gleam, intense and vivid, was gathered up the light of all His years. Here in one action, which we name His dying, was gathered up the love in which He worked. And it is just because of the power of that action…Christ could say, "And I, when I am lifted up from the earth, will draw all people to Myself." We see how true this is as a fact of history in the story of the Christian Church. There is the closest connection in that story between the death of Christ and missionary zeal. There have been periods in the Church's history when the death of Christ was practically hidden. The message of the cross was rarely preached; the meaning of the cross was rarely grasped. And the gospel was looked on as a refined philosophy, eminently suited for the good of people, instilling a most excellent morality, and in perfect harmony with human reason. We have had periods like that in Scotland, and we have had periods like that in England. God grant that they may never come again with their deadening of true religion. And always when you have such a period, when love is nothing and moral law is everything, you have a period when not a hand is lifted for the salvation of the heathen world. For it is not morality that seeks the world; it is religion centering in love. It is a view of a divine love so wonderful that it stooped to the service of death upon a cross. So always, in evangelical revival, when that has been understood in the wonder of it, the passion to tell about it has come again, and people have carried the message to the world...

To realize what it means that Christ died is to have a gospel that we must impart. There are many excellent people who, in their secret heart, confess to a very faint interest in missions. They give, and it may be that they give generously, and yet in their hearts they know that they are not interested. They know almost nothing about mission fields, and are never seen at missionary meetings, and take the opportunity to visit a sister church when a missionary is advertised to preach in theirs. With such people I have no lack of sympathy, for I think I understand their position thoroughly. I have the gravest doubt if any good is done by trying passionately to stimulate their interest. But I am perfectly confident that these good people would awaken to a new and lively interest if only they realized a little more about the wonder of the love of God in Christ...At one time the God who is eternal stooped down from heaven and came into humanity, and bore our burdens, and carried our sorrows, and died in redeeming love upon the cross. Realize once what that means, and everything else in the world is insignificant. Realize once what that means, and you must pass it on to other people. And that is the source of missionary zeal—not blind obedience, nor any thoughts of terror—but the passing on of news so wonderful that we cannot—dare not—keep it to ourselves.

The Cross and the World: Part 2 of 2
by George H. Morrison

(http://devotionals.ochristian.com/george-h-morrison-devotional-sermons-complete.shtml)

"And I, when I am lifted up from the earth, will draw all people to Myself."
John 12:32

The Answer for a Universal Need

In the next place, the death of Christ interprets and answers a universal longing. It perfectly satisfies the deepest need of all the world. One of the great gains of this age of ours is that it has drawn the world together to such a degree. There is now an intermingling of the nations that but a few decades ago was quite impossible. Thanks to the means of transportation we possess, and to the need of expansion on the part of nations; thanks to the deathless spirit of adventure, to the gains of commerce and to the march of armies, there is a blending now of the whole earth such as was undreamed of once. Now one result of all that intermingling has been a new sense of the oneness of humanity. No longer do we delight in travelers' tales, such as captivated the Middle Ages. People push their way into untraveled forests, and they come to us from Arabia and Tibet…they bring us tidings of the touch of nature that makes the whole world related. We realize today, as people have never before, how God has made all nations of one blood. Deeper than everything that separates us, there are common sorrows and essential hopes. There is one common heart by which we live; one common life in which we share; one common enemy awaiting all…

But especially this oneness of humanity has been made evident in the religious life. That has been one incalculable gain of the modern study of comparative religion. It has investigated a thousand rituals, and found at the back of them a common longing. It has touched the foundations of a thousand altars, and found they were built upon a common need. It has gathered from Africa, from India, and from China the never-failing story of religion, and always at the very heart of things it has discovered one unchanging element. It is not enough to say that all people have religion. That is now an accepted fact. Something far more wonderful and thrilling has been slowly emerging into prominence. It is that under a thousand different rituals...lies the unquenchable desire of individuals to get into a right relationship with God. Deeper than all sense of gratitude, deeper than unreasoning terror—the deepest longing in the soul of a person is the longing to get right with God. It is that in the last analysis which explains sacrifice. It is that which explains the sway of heathen witchcraft, of which the evils can never be exaggerated. The religious life is the deepest life of man, and in that life...the one determining and vital question is: how can a mortal get right with God?...

That very question...is the question which the atonement answers. It answers the cry that is rising up to the heavens from every heathen ritual and heathen altar. It tells people in language that a child can grasp, yet with a depth that angels cannot comprehend, how sinful people—by an appointed sacrifice—can be put right with the eternal God. I believe with all my soul in educational missions, but at the heart of missions there is more than education. I believe with all my soul in medical missions, but at the heart of missions there is more than healing. Christ never said, "My teaching shall draw all people," nor yet, "My healing power shall draw all people"; He said, "I, if I be lifted up, shall draw all people, and this He spoke of the death that He should die." That means that in the atoning death there is the answer to everyone's deepest need. It means that the deepest cry of all humanity is answered in the message of the cross...

DAY 7
Giants Wanted: Part 1 of 3
by Ernest A. Kilbourne
(Excerpted from *The Great Commission*, published by Oriental Missionary Society,
Tokyo, Japan in 1913)

"The voice of your brother's blood is crying to Me from the ground."
Genesis 4:10

...O how Satan will fight to keep the importance of the Great Commission in the shade! He will dim the eyes of the saints and hinder them from looking on the great fields lying in dense heathen darkness across the seas until their indifference becomes a great grief to the Holy Ghost. Of course Satan hates divine healing, and hates the fact of the second coming, and every other blessed truth of God's Word; but above all things he so hates the cause of foreign missions, especially in the hands of Holiness people, that he has turned all the powers of hell against them to stop the battle before it reaches the shores of heathendom. One does not have far to look to ascertain how well he has succeeded. Holiness missionaries are scarce, and Holiness missionary societies are few and far between. Let us pray that God will press the missionary cause so hard upon the existing Holiness associations everywhere that they will groan aloud and go down before God in repentance for their criminal neglect. The very idea of making the missionary cause of so little importance as to give it only one day in a two-week camp meeting must be a sad sight to the innumerable witnesses who are watching this battle from the fortifications of heaven; it must be a cause for heartache to our Great Commissioner; and the angels no doubt are wondering at the utter inconsistency of such conduct on the part of the under-officers in charge on earth.

O God!...What does this seeming disregard mean for the perishing millions going down to Christless graves without knowledge? Why are so many of your children so blinded by the powers of hell that they cannot see beyond their own little "Jerusalem"? O, we pray, Heavenly Father, that You would so startle many of them by Your electric touch that they will be quickened in body, soul and spirit; and so clarified in their vision that they can see across the seas, and get a glimpse of the multitudes marching down to eternal despair, whom they must face at the judgment and answer why they withheld the Bread of Life. Put such overwhelming burdens upon Your children in the homelands for the regions beyond that they shall be compelled to go, give or send as never before, that the thousands of open doors of these dark lands may be quickly entered; that the eager hands outstretched to receive the Bread of Life may not go to the grave empty; and that the strongholds of Satan may crumble and fall at the blast of the trumpets of those pushed out to face the enemy in the farthest parts.

God is looking for committed people these latter days who can put their shoulder to the wheel...people who do not fail nor let down, but who go through the shrieking hosts of hell with their faces set like a stone and their banners unsoiled by the grime of battle; people that demons do not know what to do with, who have such a sweep of victory in their lives and ministry that the battalions of hell are perplexed as to know where to look for the next move; people of Hebrews 11 faith who move mountains and uproot trees, subdue kingdoms and grow courageous in every fight...people who can face the missionary question and not turn away, who can view the millions of heathendom and say, "Let us go up at once, and possess it; for we are well able to overcome it" [Numbers 13:30]; people who do not count their lives dear to themselves until "every creature" has heard the gospel; people of love and people of tears.

DAY 8
Giants Wanted: Part 2 of 3
by Ernest A. Kilbourne
(Excerpted from *The Great Commission*, published by Oriental Missionary Society, Tokyo, Japan in 1913)

"The voice of your brother's blood is crying to Me from the ground."
Genesis 4:10

Yes, God wants to find a few people who have died to all personal interests, who have so launched out from self and all self-desire that they are blind to everything but to do God's will and carry out His plan for the evangelization of a lost world; people of one aim and purpose in life, so dominated by Christ, so submissive and controlled by the Holy Ghost, so conquered by God, that all else is considered to be manure that we may know Christ and the power of His resurrection, and be an instrument in the hand of God Almighty for any service, at any time, in any land, under any circumstances.

Weaklings always frustrate the forward march of any army; "be no longer children" is God's order and invitation, come out of your childish ways and put on the whole armor of God. His cause has been hurt and frustrated by weaklings and childishness to such an extent that Satan has captured whole nations, yes, whole continents, and is peopling hell with more than 30,000,000 souls a year. Hundreds of Christians in the homelands are so busy tinkering with their own experience, digging it up to see if it has roots, running here and there after every wind of doctrine, and spending their money for that which is not bread either for their own souls or the souls of the heathen, that we need not wonder at the wreck and ruin which Satan has been enabled to accomplish in the ends of the earth. With Isaiah and with [George] Knapp we feel the need to cry out "Awake! Awake!!" for these are latter days and the awful rage of Satan is in the earth.

O for the thunderous tones of an archangel that we might awaken the Church to a realization of her tremendous responsibility to buy up the opportunities wide open to her in all the ends of the earth today! Somehow we feel that God is trying to get a message through to His people concerning the ripeness of the fields and the shortness of the time; and that by many providential circumstances He is speaking, but our ears are hard of hearing, the spiritual atmosphere is heavy and His signals are not heard.

We feel a great pressure upon our souls as though God was bearing down upon us with some great desire in His heart for the evangelization of the dark places of the earth these last momentous days. We hardly know how to express in words this feeling, but whenever we go to our knees for a lost world, this burden is heavy upon us and compels us to write and lift up our voice to try and cause His people to see the ripened fields of the Orient awaiting the "beautiful feet" of the gospel messenger, and we are cramped in spirit by the feebleness of all our efforts to present these tremendous facts. It somehow seems to us that God is overshadowing the Church today as though He longed to break through with thunderous tones from the heavens to startle into activity His sleeping ones—"Awake!...for some have no knowledge of God." He would gladly write the words upon the skies! But what more can He do than He has done to stir His people! He does not want our unwilling service, so He does not scare us into obedience. But O how He pleads! Through His Word, through His provisions, through His preparations, through His missionaries and through the Macedonian cry of all heathendom, the pleading voice of our God and Savior is heard again and again—"Go ye," "Go ye," "Go ye"! But His voice is drowned, His heart-throb ignored by a drowsy, worldly Church. Reclining on her couch at ease, the vision of lost souls fades away in the misty distance. The opportunity passes, is lost forever, and souls go on down to death and hell unloved, unsought.

DAY 9
Giants Wanted: Part 3 of 3
by Ernest A. Kilbourne
(Excerpted from *The Great Commission*, published by Oriental Missionary Society, Tokyo, Japan in 1913)

"The voice of your brother's blood is crying to Me from the ground."
Genesis 4:10

The signals from the *Titanic* were ignored by the *Californian* and the means for rescue were made inactive and useless by disregard, causing hundreds to perish who might have been saved. Let the *Titanic* represent the heathen world in distress sending up her signals and cries, and let the *Californian* represent the Church all wrapped up in herself, fearful of her own danger, seeking only her own safety, disregarding the Macedonian cry, forgetful of her assignment, merciless! What a vivid picture has been given us in the late disaster of what is taking place in the religious world today! God is surely signaling His Church through the distress of the heathen world as never before, but His calls are mostly ignored, and millions perish whose souls might have been saved.

We are told that certain atmospheric conditions make it very difficult for radio signals to be received, and that at such times there is a confusion of sounds and the real messages are misinterpreted or lost entirely. And it seems to us that there is just such an atmospheric condition in the spiritual world today that closes the ear to the voice of God, and shuts out the true message, or distorts it into meaningless words, for how else may we account for the ignored assignment to go to "every creature" with the glad tidings of great joy? Are not His words "go ye" misinterpreted to mean someone else and not I? Are not His words "all the world" translated to convey a very different meaning? Have not the blurred signals changed the importance of His "every creature" to a meaningless command? And until the spiritual atmosphere is cleared by the baptism with the Holy Ghost and fire, His messages will mean almost anything! "Go ye" will sound like "Go he" or "Go she"—the personal element will drop out or change and shift to others. "All the world" will diminish into "all my world" and God's field be narrowed down, all because our ears are heavy and our eyes are dim.

What does it mean, beloved, that we face such a shameful condition in the heathen world today, that after almost one hundred years of open doors these great heathen nations are mostly untouched— what does it mean? We may only hang our heads in the presence of the Great Commissioner and confess that we have miserably failed as a Church, as a people, yes, individually.

But thanks be to God we shall not continue to hang our heads, for by His grace we may "lift up the hands which hang down, and the feeble knees; and make straight paths" for the ends of the earth with the glorious gospel of the Son of God—Hallelujah!

> "Come beloved! On to the uttermost parts until
> 'every creature' has heard of our precious Jesus!
> Fling out the banner! heathen lands
> Shall see from far the glorious sight,
> And nations, crowding to be born,
> Baptize their spirits in its light!"

DAY 10
Duty of Christians to Live for the
Conversion of the World: Part 1 of 4
by Eli Smith
(Excerpted from *Missionary Sermons and Addresses*, published by Saxton & Miles,
New York, New York in 1842)

*I appeal to you therefore, brothers, by the mercies of God, to present your bodies
as a living sacrifice, holy and acceptable to God, which is your spiritual worship.*
Romans 12:1

***

Surely unspeakable gratitude must swell your hearts. And anxious to
do something in return for Him, who has done so much for you,
you will ask with Paul, "What shall I do, Lord?" To do His will must
be the command of the gratitude you owe Him…If it needed any
confirmation on your part, it has already been given. For you have
by your own act solemnly promised to be the Lord's. You cannot
escape from your obligation to do the will of your Savior. And that
will is that the spiritual welfare of our race is to be promoted, that
the world is to be converted. Every page of the Bible, every action
of the Savior, declares this to be the great wish of His heart.

The obligation is strengthened by the fact that Christians are the
only agents the Savior has appointed on earth to execute this—His
great desire. What is the simple provision He has made for the
world's conversion? By His substitutionary death He has laid a
foundation for the pardon of all who repent and believe in Him. To
produce among people this repentance and faith (the indispensable
conditions of pardon), He has provided appropriate means, has
appointed agents to use those means, and has promised an influence
from above to give them success. The means He has provided are
His word, to be applied to the mind by reading, preaching, or the
various other modes of instruction. The influence He has promised

is by giving them effectiveness through that of His Holy Spirit. But who are the agents? Some agents are needed. Without them, the means will never be applied, and of course can never be made effective, unless the gospel is preached by miracle, as it never was even in the age of miracles. Jesus is no longer Himself personally on earth, a preacher of righteousness. He never employs angels to preach the gospel. The agents He has appointed are people. And among them, the only ones He can depend upon are Christians. Yes, Christian brothers and sisters, to us He has confided this great assignment, making our cooperation necessary to the accomplishment of His purposes respecting our world, so that if we prove unfaithful, His purpose fails. How tremendously responsible is our situation!...

The obligation is still further increased by His positive command. His final charge to His Church, His last will and testament, was the command, "Go into all the world and preach the gospel to every creature." This command, from the moment it was uttered until the present hour, has been binding upon the Church. Oh the guilt of so long neglecting it!...God has done His part for the conversion of the world. He has provided the means and commanded His agents to use them; it has always been His wish that the command should be obeyed. Had it been, the work would long since have been finished. But the Church has disobeyed, and the world remains in darkness.

The continued lack of repentance is to be blamed on the sinner's own disobedience; the Church's disobedience is to blamed for the world still being unconverted...The Church is charged with the guilt of suffering, error, sin, and idolatry that pervade the earth through so many generations. And at her door will the guilt still lie, until through her awakened energies our entire race is reclaimed.

DAY 11
Duty of Christians to Live for the
Conversion of the World: Part 2 of 4
by Eli Smith
(Excerpted from *Missionary Sermons and Addresses*, published by Saxton & Miles,
New York, New York in 1842)

*I appeal to you therefore, brothers, by the mercies of God, to present your bodies
as a living sacrifice, holy and acceptable to God, which is your spiritual worship.*
Romans 12:1

And how great is this guilt? Is it so enormous that you hesitate to
accuse the Church of God? Look at her history and present
condition, and say whether God Himself has not accused her and
punished her for it too. Since the apostolic spirit, which was none
other than the spirit of missions, ceased, see how barrenness has
seized her.

Heresies, rivalries, and schisms first tore her vital organs and severed
her afflicted limbs. Some of her members, who were scattered in the
East by persecution by the followers of Muhammed, were soon
mangled, and are still trampled underfoot. Upon others in Europe
the papal palsy seized, and still holds them in the grasp of a
deathlike paralysis. The Reformation for a time aroused a part to
action. But the great business of sending the gospel to the nations
was neglected, and Germany, the land of the Reformers, now
slumbers in the apathy of wordplay. A deadly lethargy threatened to
fasten itself even upon our own churches; but in a happy hour the
spirit of missions awakened their energies, and now they are
compelled onward in a course of prosperity and advancement. In a
word, if the Church neglects her duty to the world, her whole
history shows that nothing can save her from decline and spiritual
death, inflicted as a punishment for her sin. And well it may be so;
for to allow so many millions of souls to perish, whom she is under

every possible obligation to reclaim, is a sin of great enormity. Who, by withholding their efforts from the great work of converting the world, would make themselves participants in a sin of such magnitude?

The spirit of missions is the spirit of Christianity. It should be thought of as the sun and center of the system around which all its other distinctives may revolve as primary or secondary planets. For Christianity is a religion not for you and me alone, but for the world. Its Author laid down His life for the world. It begs to be published to the world. The world, and not any one person, nor set of people, nor any nation exclusively, has a right to it. That person alone has drunk anything of its spirit who aims to give it to the world. And the more one drinks of it, the more will this be the leading aim of one's conduct; the more one will give one's self actively and wholly to the work.

But how different is this from the place previously assigned to missions? What is done for missions has been extensively regarded as something extra, or redundant, hardly entering into the essential requirements of the gospel. It might be done, or left undone, at our option. It was charity, not duty. However little might be done, it was set down as so much positive credit, not as a miserable fraction of what we ought to do, bringing us sadly in debt. In the ordinary routine of prayer, public or private, after the presentation of numerous personal requests and petitions for friends, the heathen were remembered in a single word or two for a conclusion. Monthly missions meetings were poorly attended, and in the prayers that were offered, everything else perhaps found a place before the great purpose for which those meetings were called, if that purpose was not in fact entirely neglected. In giving for the support of missions, the question very generally has been not what, in the exercise of proper activity and self-denial, can be given consistently with other obligations, but what can be given without being felt, without curtailing one's income...

DAY 12
Duty of Christians to Live for the
Conversion of the World: Part 3 of 4
by Eli Smith
(Excerpted from *Missionary Sermons and Addresses*, published by Saxton & Miles, New York, New York in 1842)

I appeal to you therefore, brothers, by the mercies of God, to present your bodies as a living sacrifice, holy and acceptable to God, which is your spiritual worship.
Romans 12:1

Ministers have also been guilty of neglecting missions with their people. How rarely have missions been preached as a regular part of that system of truth which ministers are bound to preach, whether the congregations will hear, or whether they will refuse! The apology for some special occasion has been deemed necessary in order for missions being introduced with appropriateness into the regular instructions of the sanctuary; or they have been crowded into some extra meeting in the evening, or in the week; or perhaps neglected entirely by the pastor, and left to be brought forward only by occasional agents. And then their sound was so strange that you might overhear one and another in the congregation saying to one's neighbor in tones of disappointment, "I came to hear the gospel preached, and not missions." As if the Spirit that breathed in the blessed announcement by the angels at Bethlehem, "Behold, I bring you good tidings of great joy, which shall be to all people" and which would carry that proclamation to every nation, had nothing to do with the gospel!

So long as missions continue to be thrust into a back corner by Christians, we need not wonder that the world should still lie in wickedness. Quite a different place must be assigned to missions, the place that properly is its right, before the world can be converted. Missions must be preached by ministers as a regular part of the gospel, an important portion of the message they are charged by God to deliver.

Line upon line and precept upon precept must be given regarding them, until Christians come to feel that their responsibility to the world is a duty; a duty the neglect of which brings enormous guilt; a duty binding upon every individual. Christians must equip themselves for the work, as a work appropriately theirs, and one of vast significance. Their time, talents, money must be regarded as consecrated to it, by virtue of the connection they maintain with the Savior; and must be actually given to it, as the great business of life, with the feeling that it is for this very work that they are continuing to live upon the earth. When such become the feelings and conduct of Christians, we may expect the speedy approach of the millennium kingdom. They will be its signal, as the putting out of the leaves of the fig tree indicates that summer is near. Blessed be God, some Christians of this type already exist, and their number is increasing. They are the first glimmering dawn of the latter day glory.

DAY 13
Duty of Christians to Live for the
Conversion of the World: Part 4 of 4
by Eli Smith

(Excerpted from *Missionary Sermons and Addresses*, published by Saxton & Miles,
New York, New York in 1842)

I appeal to you therefore, brothers, by the mercies of God, to present your bodies
as a living sacrifice, holy and acceptable to God, which is your spiritual worship.
Romans 12:1

Missionaries are not the only persons who are bound to make
sacrifices. The appeal is to all, that they present their bodies a living
sacrifice to God. There seems to have been in the past an
impression that while missionaries tear themselves away from the
tenderness of home, and submit to the hardships of barbarous
lands, Christians who remain at home are at liberty to seek their
comfort and gratification. It is expected of missionaries that they
will of course lead a life of self-denial, but other Christians may do
it, or not, as they choose. The whole world would cry out, and justly
too, against the missionaries who should design their plans for the
accumulation of property and for self-indulgence, but Christians at
home pursue such plans, and the world does not move its tongue.
Public opinion lays heavy burdens upon the missionaries...if the
sacrifices alluded to may be so named, but Christians at large hardly
feel the necessity of self-denial.

And is there in reality one set of obligations laid upon missionaries,
and another more lenient upon the rest of the community? Where
will you find them described? In the Bible? I do not know upon
what page. I discover no distinction made there between
missionaries and yourselves. They are not singled out by any
requirement that is not equally aimed at others.

Where is it said to them "deny yourself," and the same broad command does not rest equally upon you? The providence of God has called them indeed to go in person as missionaries and to you He may not have pointed out such a course. But has He thereby imposed upon them an obligation to self-denial from which you are exempted? Are you not bound to labor equally hard at home in the same great work? The type of self-denial laid upon you, and the place in which it is to be practiced, are different; but does not the amount pressing upon both remain the same? I really cannot find that God has imposed upon me one obligation to make more sacrifices as a missionary than others are bound to make as Christians, however different in kind our respective sacrifices may be.

I am not saying that I should not make sacrifices. I do not complain about being expected and required to make them. If I were inclined to complain, someone other than myself ought to preach to you the doctrine of this sermon. My conscience does not bring such a charge against me. I have suggested no principle which I do not regard as binding upon myself. Indeed, if what has been said may have seemed to you too close and unqualified an application of Christian obligation, and a requirement of too much, my apology is that it is a mere description of what my views of our religion have long led me to feel to be obligatory upon myself; and regarding God as no respecter of persons that He should excuse others, I have believed the same to be binding upon you, and consider it to be my duty to present it.

DAY 14
Jesus Looked, Saw and Said
by Joseph Parker
(Excerpted from his sermon "Jesus and Zacchaeus" taken from his book,
The City Temple, published by Hodder & Stoughton, London, England in 1820)

And when Jesus came to the place, He looked up, and saw him, and said
unto him, "Zacchaeus, make haste, and come down;
for today I must abide at your house."
Luke 19:5

Observe the development which is traced in this verse. Jesus Christ *looked*, *saw*, and *said*. It is possible to look without seeing; many people can look upon the crowds of the world without emotion; human history gives them no deep significance; in their eyes people are but customers, clients, patrons; the idea of immortality never mingles with their uncivil thinking. On the other hand, it is possible both to look and to see; to the highest type of mind, the sight of a crowd brings sadness of heart; every person is seen to be a mystery—to be the bearer of untold sorrow—to be weak through sin, and to be bearing the black seal of death; to such types of mind, life becomes one long sigh, by reason of the wickedness which weakens and dehumanizes the race. It is possible, however, both to look and to see, yet not to say. There is a lack of moral courage, even where there is a deep appreciation of the necessities of the situation.

Many people will tell you that when they have been brought into contact with persons of extreme depravity, they have just been on the point of preaching the gospel, yet they have abstained from speaking the Word of life. When Christians look, and see, and *say*, there will go out into the world such an evangelizing commission as has never yet sought the recovery of people. Have you ever spoken to one human creature about their personal salvation? You tell me you have looked upon your friend, and that you have seen the deepest lack of his or her life, yet you have not delivered the message of God to his or her soul. Believe me, this is not friendship...

Is it not noticeable that Jesus Christ addressed Zacchaeus by name? To the reverent mind this circumstance justly suggests the omniscience [all-knowing] of the Son of God. Did not the Lord say to Moses, "I know you by name"? We, too, are known in our individuality. If we have set ourselves in any position, ordinary or unique, for the purpose of seeing the Savior, the All-Seeing Eye is upon us, and our personal name is associated with the act. How did Zacchaeus receive the word that was addressed to him? Did he hesitate? Did he excuse himself on the ground that he had been seeking to gratify merely a natural curiosity?

Many persons take up positions of observation in the sanctuary, and when they are personally invited to active service on behalf of Jesus Christ, or closer communion with the Church, they instantly claim merely a general interest, and excuse themselves from yielding to the appeal on the most trivial grounds. They turn the sanctuary into a convenience; they make use of the perspective without any pledge of loyalty to the claims of Christ, and treat with coldness the invitations which might call their souls into a most fruitful and glorious development.

DAY 15
Enthusiasm: Part 1 of 3
by Albert B. Simpson

(Excerpted from *Earnests of the Coming Age*, published by Christian Alliance Publishing Company, New York, New York in 1921)

"I know your deeds, that you are neither cold nor hot. I wish that
you were either one or the other!"
Revelation 3:15

There are two kinds of Christians: There is the conventional Christian—orthodox, correct, and cold; and there are the glowing Christians—aflame with zeal, irregular often in their methods, less concerned about order than results, less interested in confessions of faith than in getting people to confess Christ, and every fiber of their being absorbed in the one intense business of serving their Master and saving others. Which is the Scriptural type? Which is the most needed in this strenuous age? Is there a more supreme necessity in the Church of God and the development of Christian life than divine enthusiasm and the passionate fire of love for God and the souls of all?

First Love
God demands the intense and supreme love of His people. When it comes to love, even human love, there is no place for indifference. It must either be love or lukewarmness. Christ's reproach against the church of Ephesus was, "I have this against you, that you have left your first love" [Revelation 2:4]. First love here means not the early love of the young disciple, but the love that puts Christ first. God's last message to the churches of Asia and through them to the Church of the latest age [Laodicea, specifically, but contemporary as well] is, "Because you are lukewarm, I will spit you out of My mouth; I wish that you were either cold or hot."

Self-Sacrificing Love
Even in human affairs there is no nobler passion than self-sacrificing love. Greek heroism grew invincible by dwelling on the memory of [King] Leonidas and [the battle of] Marathon [ancient Greece]. Rome cherished the patriotic legends of her early history above all other glories. The story of Horatius, the legendary, noble knight who plunged headlong with his horse into the opening gulf at the gates of Rome, which nothing else could fill, and thus laid the foundation of the capital in his own heroic self-sacrifice—these were the inspirations of Roman courage and the noblest records of her history.

***

The Effect of Self-Sacrifice Upon the Heathen
There is nothing that will so impress the world as the sight of Christian self-sacrifice. Our missionaries tell us that when they go to the foreign field that it is extremely difficult to convince the natives of China, for instance, of their unselfish motives. They cannot be persuaded that there is not some ulterior design, some mercenary purpose. They are so accustomed themselves to give nothing without its equivalent that they cannot believe in unselfish goodness. When they really do find that the Christian missionary has no motive but their good, they are completely overwhelmed, their confidence is at once established, and their own lives are lifted up with the same high devotion.

We cannot expect the world to believe us and our testimony if we are not willing to risk something for it; and undoubtedly the noble examples of our missionary heroes in patient suffering, unwearied labor, and lifelong sacrifice for the souls to whose salvation they have devoted their lives, have formed the strongest claim upon their confidence and devotion.

There will never be much power in a comfort-seeking church, a self-indulgent Christian worker and a minister that preaches about a crucified Savior without having himself shared His cross. "The marks of the Lord Jesus" are the truest badge of genuineness and power.

DAY 16
Enthusiasm: Part 2 of 3
by Albert B. Simpson

(Excerpted from *Earnests of the Coming Age*, published by Christian Alliance Publishing Company, New York, New York in 1921)

"I know your deeds, that you are neither cold nor hot. I wish that you were either one or the other!"
Revelation 3:15

There is something intensely attractive in an earnest soul. The heart of the world responds to enthusiasm in a leader. It was the passionate soul of Peter the Hermit [Amiens, France] and other enthusiasts of his day that roused the slumbering world of the Middle Ages to the most extraordinary enterprises and sacrifices for the purpose of reclaiming the cross of Jesus Christ from the hands of the infidel. Oh, for ministers, evangelists, missionaries, and men and women on fire with enthusiasm for Christ and love for perishing souls! People will begin to think about their own souls when they see our earnestness, our tears, our sacrifices.

Antidote to Selfishness
Nothing else can overcome selfishness except love...Love always transforms...

The dry rot of modern Christianity is selfishness, worldliness and love of comfort, the pursuit of pleasure, the gratification of our own desires. All this is incompatible with true love to Christ...the heart will cling to these until it is lifted out of it by a superior passion. This cannot be accomplished by the conventional type of religious life...A stronger force is needed: the more glorious and consuming flame of heavenly love...There must be a divine joy, a heavenly love, and a heart-filling service for God and others.

A Divine Passion for Souls

One of the most beautiful and practical forms of Christian enthusiasm is love for souls...The passion of soul-winning leads us to watch for souls on all occasions and at all times, and to take the most intense delight in winning them for God. It leads us to adapt ourselves to people, to study them, and to attract them through the responsive chord which we can always find in every heart. A cold, unsympathetic nature will never be used to draw souls to Christ...

Anna Shipton [England 1815-1901] very beautifully tells us of her vision of heaven, how one night as she lay down, weary in her work, she longed that she might wake in heaven. She fell asleep and dreamed that she was sailing into the harbor of heaven through a sea of glass, and numerous loved ones were standing on the shore to welcome her. But looking around, she noticed that the waters were filled with drowning men and women and children who were reaching out their hands with despairing cries for her to save them. Immediately she lifted up her face to the beautiful city and said: "Father, I do not ask You to take me to that blessed heaven, but rather send me back to save those lost ones." Then it seemed to her that the very cords of her heart were loosened and became cables as she swam through the sea, and the drowning ones clung to her very heartstrings as she painfully drew them home, and the water around her was stained crimson from her own heart with the agony of her love.

It was thus that the Master sought and saved us. It was no easy task for the Shepherd to seek and find His lost ones, but love made it a delight. It was the reproach of His enemies, "And the Pharisees and scribes murmured, saying, 'This man receives sinners, and eats with them.'" Of His journey to Samaria it is said, "He must go through Samaria," and the reason was that a poor lost woman was waiting at Jacob's well for His messages of love. His last act on the cross was to stretch out His hands and take with Him to Paradise a dying criminal, and still through the Holy Spirit He is ever seeking and saving the lost with wearied and patient love...This is the secret of all successful evangelistic work: a deep, intense desire for souls.

DAY 17
Enthusiasm: Part 3 of 3
by Albert B. Simpson
(Excerpted from *Earnests of the Coming Age*, published by Christian Alliance Publishing Company, New York, New York in 1921)

"I know your deeds, that you are neither cold nor hot. I wish that
you were either one or the other!"
Revelation 3:15

The Secret of Missionary Success
The same passionate love of souls is the source of the missionary's power. Nothing else will ever make us happy or effective among the unpleasant surroundings of a heathen land. But to the true soul-winner all considerations of personal comfort, pleasant surroundings, of even apparent success are forgotten in the one thought, "There are immortal beings here to be lost or saved." Someone was telling such a person of the discomforts of heathen lands: "There are scorpions there; there are deadly snakes there; there is scorching heat there; there are cruel and murderous savages there." But finally he asked: "Are there people there?" "Yes, there are millions of them." Then the answer was: "Where there are people I must go and seek and save them."

Dr. [Alexander] Duff was an example of missionary enthusiasm. It was a splendid spectacle to see the old veteran as he pleaded for India and begged the young men and women of Scotland to go out to that needy field. Once in a great meeting in the General Assembly Hall he fainted in the middle of his address, and they carried him to the back room unconscious. In a little while he recovered and begged to be taken back. "You will die if you do," they said. And the old hero answered: "I'll die if I don't. I must go and ask the young men of Scotland if there is nobody left but me to go back and tell the millions of India of the love of Jesus." It was this intense enthusiasm that led [David] Livingstone to traverse the Dark Continent and to live and die with one supreme ambition: to heal the open sore of Africa.

It was this that sustained [Alexander Murdoch] McKay amid the awful perils and trials of the early days of Uganda. It was this that kept the martyrs of China at their posts throughout the awful days of the Boxer rebellion [1900] until hundreds of them confirmed their testimony with their blood. It was this that enabled Pastor Harms, Pastor Gossner and Count Zinzendorff and the Moravians to count every earthly thing as waste as they sent out the first pioneers of the gospel to the snows of Labrador and the scorching suns of Africa and India. It is this divine enthusiasm in human hearts and lives that today is pressing forward into every open door in the Philippines, in Puerto Rico, in China, and in Tibet.

There is no more splendid passion than the love of souls, and especially the love of countless lost heathen souls. Even Francis Xavier [1502-1556], with all the faults and errors of the Catholic Church, was honored by the missionary passion, and there is no more splendid record in Christian history than the life of this apostle of love, sweeping over the world like the Apocalyptic "angel flying in the midst of heaven having the everlasting gospel to preach to all that dwell upon the face of the earth," until at last he sank dying there over against the shores of China, crying with his final breaths: "O rock, will you never open to my Lord?" The missionary enthusiasm is reviving in the Church of God. Let us fan its rising flame, let us kindle it afresh in the hearts of our children, our students, our friends, until it sets on fire the slumbering Church of God...

DAY 18
Passages from Letters and Messages: Part 1 of 4
by Matthew T. Yates
(Excerpted from *The Story of Yates the Missionary* by Charles E. Taylor, published
by Sunday School Board of the Southern Baptist Convention,
Nashville, Tennessee in 1898)

Shanghai, May 24, 1868
I am doing what I can in our mission work. The people come to
hear me preach, but will not turn from their sins and idols. Many of
them become more or less interested, but it is too often like the
morning dew. As I am now prepared for this work, I suppose that it
is my duty to continue in it. The field is the world, and this is, by far,
the largest field on the face of the globe. China does not look large
on the map—but the people—there are four hundred million here,
and all going the downward road. It seems to be the will of the Lord
that I should wear out here.

Shanghai, December, 1868
Our religion is attracting the attention of the intellectuals and
officials. The power of the gospel of Christ is making itself felt in
China. The thinking classes are not slow to see that it aims at an
entire subversion of their ancient systems. Opposition will not injure
our cause. It will only attract attention to the new religion, as, in days
gone by, it has done in the West.

Shanghai, December 31, 1868
My church is growing in knowledge, and in some cases greatly in
efficiency. My idea of a properly trained church is that every
member should feel that he or she has a work to do for the
conversion of others. Never have I felt more certain of the ultimate
triumph of the gospel in China.

The following are notes from a message delivered at a Missionary Conference (date and place unknown):
To secure an [evangelistically] aggressive native church, there are some things which I regard as fundamental:

1. A converted and evangelical membership. To admit another element into our churches, even though they may be persons of wealth or influence as scholars, is to paralyze the whole church. The persons of wealth and influence will give the moral tone to the church.

2. They should be taught that, when they embrace Christianity, they become the disciples of Jesus Christ and not the disciples of the missionary.

3. As they have become the disciples of Jesus, they should become thoroughly acquainted with His teachings in the language in which they think and speak. They should be encouraged to commit to memory precious and practical portions of the New Testament in the spoken language of their particular locality.

4. They should be taught the individuality of their religion—that they are personally responsible to God; that they can and ought to exert a personal influence in behalf of the religion which they profess.

We need to take hold and show them how it should be done; this will be easy to do, for the Chinese are good imitators, and example is a good teacher. And at first, if they need a little aid, we should render it, for nothing is so encouraging as success. We should strive to avoid the depressing influence of failure. And let it be ever borne in mind that we need not expect our native preachers to be aggressive unless we are aggressive ourselves.

Shanghai, April 24, 1869
At my morning service every seat was occupied by very attentive hearers. While preaching, I saw tears flowing freely from the eyes of more than one. This is an unusual sight in a heathen congregation.

DAY 19
Passages from Letters and Messages: Part 2 of 4
by Matthew T. Yates
(Excerpted from *The Story of Yates the Missionary* by Charles E. Taylor, published
by Sunday School Board of the Southern Baptist Convention,
Nashville, Tennessee in 1898)

Shanghai, May 9, 1869

I asked our native preacher, Wong, a few weeks ago how he would explain the apparent change of feeling in our congregation. He replied: "Your preaching goes to the heart now: formerly it only went in at one ear and out at the other. You preach much better than in former years."

Shanghai, May 17, 1869

And still they come. Yesterday I baptized two more. Others are waiting for the opposition of friends to cease. While the churches at home seem to have utterly forsaken me and my work, the Lord is verifying His promise, "I am with you." It costs the Chinese, especially women, something to become Christians. I am delighted with the spirit of the late converts. After more than twenty-one years of labor, I have reached the Chinese heart. Oh, there is joy in my little church. My church, of believers only, is attracting more and more attention. There seems to be something in the simple act of immersion that impresses the Chinese favorably. It carries with it the idea of truthfulness and stability.

Shanghai, September 12, 1877

At first the way was in the dark; but every successive decade has shown marked progress in our work. Today the missionary influence in China is a mighty power...Thirty years ago, when the prospect was so dark, and the darkness seemed so impenetrable, I would have compromised for what I now behold as my life work. Now, my demand would be for nothing less than a complete surrender. I fully realize that God is in Christ reconciling the world to Himself; He has committed to us the word of reconciliation; and He has commanded us to make it known among all nations…I rejoice that He has counted me worthy to be His ambassador to the greatest empire on the globe.

Shanghai, November 7, 1880
This has been a glorious day with me. At 9:30 I preached in English at my new church on the Great Commission. Then I baptized three men—an Englishman, a Swede, and an American. They said that they were not satisfied with their baptism in infancy, and wished to obey Christ—believe, and then be baptized.

At 10:30 I took the pulpit again and preached to a house full of Chinese. After the sermon, we had a good communion time. This occupied my time until 12 o'clock. Then I went to my room, and, after earnestly asking God's blessing on the labors of the day, I sat alone in sweet meditation upon that precious promise, "And lo, I am with you always," and upon the trustworthiness of Christ in fulfilling His promises. My cup of blessing ran over, and—oh, well, I just had a good swim in the love of God. The cup of blessing is so near to every Christian, and yet how few ever partake of it.

Shanghai, December, 1882
It is a melancholy fact that a large number of missionaries from England and America fail to accomplish the professed object of their mission. During my term of long service, I have witnessed many sad failures. I fear that the underlying cause was a mistaken call to the work. The divine call, I would say, is a growth and not a sudden excess of feeling called for by a stirring appeal. The latter is too short-lived for the stern realities of aggressive missionary life. Nor is the call acquired at schools of learning. It is the gift of God in answer to the prayer, "What will You have me do?" Some come out under a meteoric call. They have entertained emotional and romantic views of the work among the heathen, and, when they come into contact with the objects of their compassion and find the work different from what they expected, they soon become disgusted with themselves and their surroundings.

DAY 20
Passages from Letters and Messages: Part 3 of 4
by Matthew T. Yates

(Excerpted from *The Story of Yates the Missionary* by Charles E. Taylor, published by Sunday School Board of the Southern Baptist Convention, Nashville, Tennessee in 1898)

Shanghai, February, 1883

As today is Chinese New Year, when all, from the Emperor down, claim a holiday, and while hundreds of thousands, dressed in their best, are walking the streets, cracking watermelon, pumpkin, sunflower, and other seeds, I will take my recreation in writing to my very dear friend.

I have just revised and put to press an edition of Mark and Luke in the Shanghai [Chinese] dialect. The four Gospels, Acts, and Romans are now in the hands of the people. I use Alford's Greek text. It is surprising to find that many translators into English, as well as into Chinese, have allowed their theological views to influence and mar their translations. Oh, how I would like to have a few hours to talk with Broadus, Boyce, and others. You can see how important it is that a candidate for the China missions should be thoroughly furnished.

An hour and a half is spent each morning with my class of three young student assistants. They commit everything to memory. This has been hard on them and on me too, but it has made new men and good preachers of them. For, if a man has nothing to say, he can say nothing worth hearing. I have done good work with these men; the result will go on down the ages, long after I am laid aside.

Homiletics [the skill of preaching] has not claimed much of my attention. The Chinese do not understand, but are bewildered and frightened by any attempt at oratory. In 1868, just before my voice gave way, I was preaching on the second coming of Christ, and had more than my usual "liberty." I perceived that my congregation was in an anxious state of mind. Why, I could not tell. Some, who were not members of the church, bolted out of the house, declaring that I made the little dog within them bite. Many church members were standing up and wringing their hands. At this juncture, an old sister walked up to my pulpit and putting her hands over my Bible exclaimed: "Stop, He is coming, and we are all frightened to death!" I saw what the matter was, and turned their thoughts to the joys of those who should be ready at His coming. The old sister returned to her seat saying: "That is the kind I like."

From the time of Abraham until now, the Chinese have not been accustomed to public speaking. Their speakers sit down and talk like a judge on the bench, and make gestures with their fans. I have learned to use one too. So, if I am ever permitted to enter your pulpit in warm weather, you must allow me to take my fan and use it too; and no one is to be permitted to smile. And if I should inadvertently break info speaking Chinese, you must pull my coat tail, or your people would laugh at me. You will see from the rough chart which I send you that I am projecting and laying out work for several generations of missionaries. Before now, we have "cultivated," say, a hundred acres only. My program "encloses" ten thousand acres. When I stood on the top of the hill in Kwinsan, a few days ago, I thought of the Savior weeping over Jerusalem and shuddered as I contemplated the jungle of humanity, the fifty million in this plain of the Yang-tsz, who care no more for *Ya-soo* (Jesus) than the Jews did for Him who wept over them. A weighty responsibility rests upon you pastors at home. All around the globe, the great lack today is people, live people, whose aim is to live for God and humanity. Those people who devote much thought to their clothing, their comforts, their social position, and the impression they are making are devoted to themselves. Few are ready to exercise the grace of working and giving and suffering. Many avoid the posts of greatest need, and seek positions of personal ease and comfort. The position desired by every truly devoted heart is where service is most needed in the kingdom of Christ.

DAY 21
Passages from Letters and Messages: Part 4 of 4
by Matthew T. Yates
(Excerpted from *The Story of Yates the Missionary* by Charles E. Taylor, published by Sunday School Board of the Southern Baptist Convention, Nashville, Tennessee in 1898)

Chefoo, September 17, 1885

The small field that I have staked off and am trying to "cultivate" embraces a population much greater than that of all the Southern States. All of this multitude, so far as the knowledge of God and of the way of life is concerned, is in total darkness. Having no knowledge of the light of revelation, they have no idea of the prosperity or misery of an immortal soul. In fact, they have no correct ideas of an immortal soul. Their own theory is heathenism, pure and simple, without enough light to produce a doubt as to the utility of their own religious systems.

This view of the residence of cruelty, where Satan reigns, may serve to give a more definite idea of the enormous work that Christ has committed to us and, at the same time, to show how inadequate the methods and means now in use are among our pastors and churches in Christian lands.

The work does look appalling to everything but faith in God and in the omnipotence [all-power] of the Holy Spirit over the human heart. But, with faith in Christ as our leader, we can accomplish wonders for the glory of God, even among these dry bones. But the faith that does not prompt one to action in behalf of Christ's cause in all lands is a dead faith. The Chinese have, and have had for ages, a civilization of their own, but it is rotten at the core. They have more gods or objects of worship than there are people in the United States. But they have had no knowledge of God for a hundred generations, and from a period beyond the start of authentic history, they have been sitting in the region and shadow of death.

Shanghai, October 20, 1887

What a fuss you all make about my going home. You talk as if it were an easy matter. Do you not know that the great globe is between us, and that it is no small matter to go from China to Raleigh, [North Carolina] to say nothing of the expense? I received your invitation to go home for a rest in July, a week or two after I was cut down by partial paralysis. One-half of me would not obey me. At that time, and for some time afterward, I was not able to go. Little by little I became able to walk. Now I can walk a mile; but it is not natural. I am weakened all over, and can fall down as easy as falling off a log. I have preached for two Sundays since we came back from Chefoo, but I was used up by it. I am not fit for work. If I to go to the States, every preacher in the land would want me to address or preach to his people. And seeing me look stout and strong, they would laugh at the idea of my not being able to do it. They would not take no for an answer. The only way I could get rid of them would be to insult them; and that I would not do. So you see, I am afraid of my friends. And what home have I in this world but this in Shanghai in winter and Chefoo in summer? Here I can control my time and have no one to harass me to do what I am not able to do.

I am required to keep quiet, as I am liable to provoke another stroke of paralysis, and this might be fatal. If I get well enough to work and hold on for another year, I shall not go to the States, for the bottom is dropping out of our missions. [Elijah E.] Davault died on the 4th; Joiner must go home this winter. Mr. and Mrs. Graves of Canton go home in the spring. Miss Moon and I are invited to go home. That looks like breaking up our missions. And we see nothing of any reinforcements to take the places of those who must go. Now, can you not see how difficult it is for me to leave Shanghai? And that is all that I can tell you about my going home soon. Moreover, I have no home in America to go to. There are forty-nine reasons why I ought to stay at home. For I am old now, you know, and need a great deal of nursing.

DAY 22
Prayerful Giving
by Ernest A. Kilbourne
(Excerpted from *The Great Commission*, published by Oriental Missionary Society, Tokyo, Japan in 1913)

Prayerful giving to the cause of Christ seems very essential these days when appeals are coming from all sides, and many are at a loss to know just where to place their offerings. It is a God-given instinct that causes us to be careful and prayerful to put money where it will bring the greatest return in treasure stored up in Heaven. When we have "died dead" to the love of filthy riches, and our only desire is to glorify God, keep a single eye, and seek the lost in all the ends of the earth, then and only then are we in line with God's financial plan for His children and in a place where we are sure of Divine guidance if we stay long enough on our knees to get it. We firmly believe that God would have His children study to give intelligently; that they should survey the field, acquaint themselves with the conditions and needs of various claims, and know that they are placing His money where He would have it placed. We should make use of every means to get knowledge concerning the needs of the various fields, and then with this knowledge go to our knees and ask God's guidance as to what use we shall put the money He has entrusted to us. In this assurance our giving will be effective: it will accomplish what God intended it should, it will bring results, there will be a calm, settled conviction that we are in the will of God, and rich blessing shall return upon our own head—praise God!

Were it possible to compute and publish the amount of useless and wasteful giving that results from prayerless and haphazard administration of God's money, no doubt we would all be sorrowfully amazed...but it surely is appropriate for us as God's children to seek His guidance in all our services—there is no other sure way. If we follow any person or any [mission] board we still need God's approval upon it, or we may drift into lifeless, uninterested, formal giving that brings no blessing, and that accomplishes little or nothing toward the evangelization of a lost world. Impulsive giving, when the impulse is from the Lord, is good and effective; but when the impulse is merely convenient, or because some appeal creates an urge at the moment, it becomes a haphazard shot—it may hit the mark, or it may not. Generally it does not. This is not God's best thought for us. Giving which is based upon our deepest convictions worked in us upon our knees by the Holy Ghost is the kind that counts. We might label it "tested giving," that is to say, we have sought and found God's thought for our offerings, we have given our money, we have seen it bring results, we have been blessed in the transaction. Surely this "tested giving" is God's plan for us! Surely it will count most in bringing about God's great purpose to make known to "every creature" His love in Christ Jesus!

Tested giving then is based upon prayer and knowing God's will and confirming it; and each one of us may be assured in our own heart concerning the grace of giving. "Each one must give as he has decided in his heart, not reluctantly or under compulsion, for God loves a cheerful giver" [2 Corinthians 9:7], is God's plan. That "heart purpose" should be worked in by the Holy Ghost, and if God's people would wait upon Him long enough with this purpose it would soon happen that there would be no more useless and wasteful giving, "for the ministry of this service [giving] not only fills up the measure of the needs of the saints, but abounds also through many thanksgivings to God" [2 Corinthians 9:12]—it is effective and full of blessing, praise God! We are quite safe in saying that it is the desire of God that all His children should make this ministry of giving a matter for much prayer, and more especially so these last days when a great effort should be exerted to reach "every creature" with the good news of salvation, that the coming of the Lord may be accelerated.

DAY 23
Holding the Ropes
by Ernest A. Kilbourne
(Excerpted from *The Great Commission*, published by Oriental Missionary Society, Tokyo, Japan in 1913)

I was let down in a basket through a window in the wall...
2 Corinthians 11:33

No mention is made of the helping hands that lowered Paul to a place of safety, but that there were hands, we are quite sure, and they were true rope-holders who did their work well. Too often we are liable to forget the ones hidden away who hold the ropes that bring deliverance to God's warriors. Too often we are liable to forget or underestimate the important part that these hidden ones are taking in God's purpose. They are an especially important part of His purpose in the "regions beyond." Little could be accomplished without the aid of those hands that let down the basket from the window. Praise God, they are loving hands! Some people who have an abnormal idea of the life of faith would tell us to cut the rope and have no connection with rope-holders, but let God do it all. No doubt God could do it all and take care of all the missionaries without the intercession of any homeland saints, but He is not working that way, for He wants all His children to have a partnership in the rescue of the lost of heathendom...

There is just as much need for the rope-holder as there is for the one at the front. This has always been God's plan through the ages ever since Paul and Barnabas, the first Christian missionaries, were sent out by the church at Antioch and supported by their prayers and gifts. They were true rope-holders at Antioch, and Paul and Barnabas were true faith missionaries, whose trust was in the living God and whose faith took hold for the supply of every need. Of course they believed God would supply their needs through those who knew them and who sent them out. This would be the natural foundation for their faith unless, indeed, Barnabas sold another field to meet the expenses of that first missionary journey. But some people today say that it is not faith when the needs are mentioned to anyone but God. This seems to be a very short-sighted view of faith, and we believe that Paul returned to Antioch and Jerusalem for the very purpose of presenting the needs of the foreign fields to the home church (see Acts 14:26-28 and 21:19). This being the case, Paul would have to be eliminated from the list of faith missionaries. But we prefer to keep him at the top as our example of a true faith missionary.

Someone has recently said that the late J. Hudson Taylor of the China Inland Mission did not run to England and America to present the needs of China; but that is a great mistake, for he made several trips, both to England and America, to Canada and to Australia for that very purpose, and his work in China was more widely known than perhaps any other missionary work, and he was nonetheless a true faith missionary. When he looked to God for the supply of a need, he knew that God would talk to those who knew of that work in China, in order to answer his prayers, so there was a necessity for a wide circle of acquaintance in all the homelands, and agents appointed in England, Australia, Canada and the United States, and three papers published in the same interest...We must not look to the rope-holder, however, but to God alone. Still we do not forget that God will assuredly use those who know about us, and are in sympathy with us, and are burdened for us in prayer, and co-laboring together with us on behalf of lost souls. These are no less true soldiers because they are standing by the supplies; no, they are just as necessary as any other part of the army. So, beloved, let us get a Scriptural view of faith, and a charitable view of faith-workers, and set a good example for all, by being a true follower of Paul as he was of Jesus Christ, who gave up all to come down to earth seeking the lost!

DAY 24
The Worldwide Gospel: Part 1 of 2
by George H. Morrison

(http://devotionals.ochristian.com/george-h-morrison-devotional-sermons-complete.shtml)

"Go into all the world, and preach the gospel to every creature."
Mark 16:15

The Gospel Deep and Wide

There are two directions in which the influence of Jesus is without any parallel in human history. One of them is that of depth; the other that of breadth. All great movements may be judged extensively—that is, by the area which they cover; or, on the other hand, they may be judged intensively by their power of influence over the individual, and in both respects, the gospel of our Lord stands quite alone upon the page of history—it is unequalled in its depth and in its breadth. The one name for the followers of Socrates was the name of disciple, or of learner. That word—disciples—was often on the lips of Christ, and is familiar on the gospel page. But it is very significant that, as the days went by, and people perceived all that they owed to Christ, the name of disciple (for all its tender memories) gave way to that of servant or slave. That indicates with what a perfect mastery Jesus Christ controls the individual. His influence reaches to the depths of being, and possesses every power and every passion. Yet even more notable than that complete control is the area over which it is to reach: "Go into all the world, and preach the gospel to every creature." The two remarkable things about the gospel are that it is deep as life and wide as all the world. It is a message of redeeming power for the whole person; it is a message of redeeming power for every person. And on that latter subject I wish to speak—on the worldwide message of the gospel. First, let us look at it in its conception; next, in its accomplishment; and, lastly, in its obligation.

The Overwhelming Boldness of the Gospel in Its Conception

There are two features in this conception to which I desire to direct your thoughts, and the first is its overwhelming boldness. If you would reflect for a moment on the facts and on the circumstances that surround the facts, there is not one of you who would not be amazed at the unparalleled boldness of the Lord.

We have read of Alexander the Great conquering the world and then weeping that there were no other worlds to conquer, but Alexander was born in a king's realm, and had a mighty army to obey him. We have read of Napoleon, with his vast ambition and his dreams of a mighty empire in the East, but Napoleon also had his hardy veterans, and his ambition rose with his success.

How different from all this is Jesus Christ, who had not a single sword to back His claims, and who, in the quiet glory of His faith, believed in His worldwide empire from the first. If He had been born in Rome of Latin ancestry we might have better understood His outlook. For Rome was stretching her power into far distances and widening the horizon of her children. But Jesus Christ was born of the narrowest and most exclusive race that ever lived. Yet out of the heart of that most restrictive heritage He looked with equal eyes upon the whole world.

In every land His gospel would be preached; in every tongue His name would be proclaimed; the heavens and the earth might pass away, but His word would never pass away, and He—who was He to make these mighty claims? He was the meek and lowly man of Nazareth, whose mother had never heard the name of Plato, and whose siblings roamed a village street. Note, too, in what a natural way our Savior talked about His worldwide mission. He did not dwell on it as one might dwell on something stupendous that was overwhelming Him. But He spoke of it as quietly and simply as you and I might talk about our work, without the slightest trace of any feeling that He had taken on Him a task that was too great.

DAY 25
The Worldwide Gospel: Part 2 of 2
by George H. Morrison
(http://devotionals.ochristian.com/george-h-morrison-devotional-sermons-complete.shtml)

"Go into all the world, and preach the gospel to every creature."
Mark 16:15

***

The Gospel Is Triumphant in Spite of Forces Against It
This impression is singularly deepened when we think of the forces allied against the gospel. It had against it the power of the State, and, still more powerful, the human heart. I shall not dwell upon persecutions which fell with such terrific force upon the Church...Far more remarkable than that survival from the bitter persecution of the State is its survival from these deadlier evils that lay in their infancy on its own bosom. When I think of the heresies which divided the early Church, of her gradual decline from spirituality, of the superstition of the Middle Ages, and the widespread skepticism it caused; when I think how the Church has been torn into divisions, and how Protestant and Catholic stand apart, it is amazing to me that people should ever dream now of carrying the gospel to the world. As a matter of fact, not only do they dream it—every day they actually do it.

Never before, in all the Christian centuries, has there been such eagerness to evangelize the world. And when you think of the story of the past, with all its division and all its degradation, that glowing zeal of the Christian Church today is a mighty witness to the living Christ. Every power that could wreck the gospel has been brought to bear on it since it was born. It has been persecuted, ridiculed, degraded; it has been wounded by foes and by its friends. Why, brethren, if Christ is not alive, I tell you that all that is unexplainable.

I pity with all my heart the men or women who say they do not believe in foreign missions; they are shutting their hearts to such a splendid proof of the divinity of Jesus Christ. "Go into all the world, and preach the gospel to every creature," and people are doing it to this very hour. To me, knowing the past, that is unexplainable unless the speaker was the Son of God…

The Accomplishments of the Gospel Put Us Under Obligation

I hear of some who believe in home missions, but have no interest in foreign missions. That attitude, I believe, is often due to lack of imagination rather than of heart. But remember, if a thousand years ago the Church had taken a position of that kind, we would still be living in a heathen country, and without a single hope in Jesus Christ. It is to the foreign missions of the past that we owe our highest life today. We are indebted for the Christian faith to people who left their home and country…But we must work to realize all that the worldwide faith has done for us; each one of us must make the verse our own if we are truly disciples of the Lord. To some there has come the call to go abroad, and they have opened their hearts to hear that call…Every one of us, whether old or young, can play a part in this unequalled labor, and help advance—more powerfully than we know—the promised evangelization of the world. I beg you, read with attention the story of that service in our missionary journals; take an intelligent interest in the matter, as I know so many of you already do; give it a large place in daily prayer, and do not be content with general petitions, but, with a mind enriched by information, intercede for particular locations. It is in such ways that we can take our place, though we may not stand in the forefront of the battle. By prayer, by interest, by thoughtful giving, we can help the worldwide triumph of the gospel. For that great victory will surely come, when the knowledge of Christ shall cover the whole earth, and the one shall be happy who, in that crowning hour, shall be found to have accelerated its coming.

DAY 26
A Short Review of Former Undertakings for the Conversion of the Heathen: Part 1 of 3
by William Carey

(Excerpted from An Enquiry into the Obligations of Christians to Use Means for the Conversion of the Heathens, published by Ann Ireland, London, England in 1792)

Thus far the history of the Acts of the Apostles informs us of the success of the word in ancient times; and history informs us of its being preached about this time, in many other places. Peter speaks of a church at Babylon; Paul proposed a journey to Spain, and it is generally believed he went there, and likewise came to France and Britain. Andrew preached to the Scythians, north of the Black Sea. John is said to have preached in India, and we know that he was at the Isle of Patmos, in the Archipelago. Philip is reported to have preached in upper Asia, Scythia, and Phrygia; Bartholomew in India, on this side the Ganges, Phrygia, and Armenia; Matthew in Arabia, or Asiatic Ethiopia [India], and Parthia [Iran]; Thomas in India, as far the coast of Coromandel, and some say in the island of Ceylon; Simon, the Canaanite, in Egypt, Cyrene, Mauritania, Libya, and other parts of Africa, and from there to have come to Britain; and Jude is said to have been principally engaged in the lesser Asia, and Greece. Their labors were evidently very extensive and very successful; so that Pliny the younger, who lived soon after the death of the apostles, in a letter to the emperor, Trajan, observed that Christianity had spread, not only through towns and cities, but also through whole countries. Indeed before this, in the time of Nero, it was so prevalent that it was thought necessary to oppose it by an Imperial Edict, and accordingly the proconsuls and other governors were commissioned to destroy it.

Justin Martyr, who lived about the middle of the second century, in his dialogue with Trypho, observed that there was no part of humankind, whether Greeks or barbarians, or any others, by whatever name they were called, whether the Sarmatians, or the Nomads, who had no houses, or the Scenites of Arabia Petrea [Arabia], who lived in tents among their cattle, where prayer and thanksgiving are not offered up to the Father, and Maker of all things, through the name of Jesus Christ. Irenaeus, who lived about the year 170, speaks of churches that were founded in Germany, Spain, France, the eastern countries, Egypt, Libya, and the middle of the world. Tertullian, who lived and wrote at Carthage [Tunisia] in Africa, about twenty years afterwards, enumerating the countries where Christianity had penetrated, makes mention of the [peoples known as Parthians [Iran], Medes [Iran], Elamites [Iran], Mesopotamians [Iraq], Armenians, Phrygians [Turkey], Cappadocians [Turkey], the inhabitants of Pontus [Turkey], Asia, Pamphylia [Turkey], Egypt, and the regions of Africa beyond Cyrene [Libya], the Romans, and Jews, formerly of Jerusalem, many of the Getuli, many borders of the Mauri, or Moors, in Mauritania; now Barbary [North Africa coast], Morocco, all the borders of Spain, many nations of the Gauls [France and parts of surrounding countries], and the places in Britain which were inaccessible to the Romans; the Dacians [Romania], Sarmatians [Iran], Germans, Scythians [Siberia], and the inhabitants of many hidden nations and provinces, and of many islands unknown to him, and which he could not enumerate. The labors of the ministers of the gospel, in this early period, were so remarkably blessed of God that the last-mentioned writer observed in a letter to Scapula, that if he began a persecution, the city of Carthage itself must be decimated thereby. Yes, and so abundant were they in the first three centuries, that ten years of constant and almost universal persecution under Diocletian could neither root out the Christians, nor prejudice their cause.

After this they were greatly encouraged under several emperors, particularly Constantine and Theodosius, and a very great work of God was carried on...

DAY 27
A Short Review of Former Undertakings for the Conversion of the Heathen: Part 2 of 3
by William Carey

(Excerpted from An Enquiry into the Obligations of Christians to Use Means for the Conversion of the Heathens, published by Ann Ireland, London, England in 1792)

In the time of Constantine, one Frumentius was sent to preach to the Indians [India], and met with great success. A young woman who was a Christian, being taken captive by the Iberians, or Georgians, near the Caspian Sea, informed them of the truths of Christianity, and was so much respected that they sent to Constantine for ministers to come and preach the word to them. About the same time some barbarous nations having invaded Thrace, carried away several Christians captive who preached the gospel; by which means the inhabitants upon the Rhine and the Danube, the Celtae [France], and some other parts of Gaul were brought to embrace Christianity. About this time also James of Nisbia went into Persia to strengthen the Christians, and preach to the heathens; and his success was so great that Adiabene [Iraq] was almost entirely Christian. About the year 372, one Moses, a monk, went to preach to the Saracens, who then lived in Arabia, where he had great success; and at this time the Goths, and other northern [European] nations, had the kingdom of Christ further extended among them, but which was very soon corrupted with Arianism [denying the divinity of Christ].

Soon after this, the kingdom of Christ was further extended among the Scythian Nomads, beyond the Danube, and about the year 430, a people called the Burgundians [Germany] received the gospel. Four years after that Palladius was sent to preach in Scotland, and the next year Patrick was sent from Scotland to preach to the Irish, who before his time were totally uncivilized, and, some say, cannibals; he, however, was useful and laid the foundations of several churches in Ireland. Presently after this, truth spread further among the Saracens, and in 522, Zathus, king of the Colchians [Egypt] encouraged it, and many of that nation were converted to Christianity. About this time also the work was extended in Ireland by Finian, and in Scotland by Constantine and Columba; the latter of whom preached also to the Picts Scotland] and Brudaeus, their king, with several others, were converted. About 541, Adad, the king of Ethiopia, was converted by the preaching of Mansionarius; the Heruli [Germany] beyond the Danube were now made obedient to the faith, and the Abafgi [Armenia, Azerbaijan, Georgia, Russia], near the Caucasian Mountains.

But now popery, especially the compulsive part of it, had risen to such a height that the usual method of propagating the gospel, or rather what was so called, was to conquer pagan nations by force of arms and then oblige them to submit to Christianity, after which bishoprics were erected and persons then sent to instruct the people. I shall just mention some of those who are said to have labored thus.

In 596, Austin, the monk, Melitus, Justus, Paulinus, and Ruffinian, labored in England, and in their way were very successful. Paulinus, who appears to have been one of the best of them, had great success in Northumberland; Birinnius preached to the West Saxons, and Felix to the East Angles. In 589, Amandus Gallus labored in Ghent [Belgium], Chelenus in Artois [France], and Gallus and Columbanus in Suabia [Germany]. In 648, Egidius Gallus in Flanders [Belgium], and the two Evaldi in Westphalia [Germany]. In 684, Willifred, in the Isle of Wight [England]. In 688, Chilianus, in upper Franconia [Germany]. In 698, Boniface, or Winifred, among the Thuringians, near Erford, in Saxony [Germany], and Willibroad in West-Friesland [Netherlands]. Charlemagne conquered Hungary in the year 800, and obliged the inhabitants to profess Christianity, when Modestus likewise preached to the Venedi, at the source of the Save and Drave [Italy]. In 833, Ansgarius preached in Denmark, Gaudibert in Sweden, and about 861, Methodius and Cyril in Bohemia [Czech Republic].

DAY 28
A Short Review of Former Undertakings for the Conversion of the Heathen: Part 3 of 3
by William Carey
(Excerpted from An Enquiry into the Obligations of Christians to Use Means for the Conversion of the Heathens, published by Ann Ireland, London, England in 1792)

About the year 500, the Scythians overran Bulgaria, and Christianity was eradicated; but about 870 they were re-converted. Poland began to be brought over about the same time, and afterwards, about 960 or 990, the work was further extended amongst the Poles and Prussians [Germany]. The work was begun in Norway in 960, and in Muscovy [Russia] in 989, the Swedes propagated Christianity in Finland in 1168, Lithuania became Christian in 1386, and Samogitia [Lithuania] in 1439. The Spaniards forced popery upon the inhabitants of South America, and the Portuguese in Asia. The Jesuits were sent into China in 1552. Xavier, whom they call the apostle of the Indians labored in the East Indies and Japan from 1541 to 1552, and several missions of Capauchins [Catholic monks] were sent to Africa in the seventeenth century. But blind zeal, gross superstition, and infamous cruelties so marked the appearances of religion all this time that the professed Christians themselves needed conversion, as much as the heathen world.

A few pious people had fled from the general corruption and lived obscurely in the valleys of Piedmont and Savoy [Italy], who were like the seed of the church. Some of them were now and then required to travel into other parts, where they faithfully testified against the corruptions of the times. About 1369 Wycliffe began to preach the faith in England, and his preaching and writings were the means of the conversion of great numbers, many of whom became excellent preachers; and a work was begun which afterwards spread in England, Hungary, Bohemia, Germany, Switzerland, and many other places. John Huss and Jerome of Prague preached boldly and successfully in Bohemia, and the adjacent parts. In the following century [Martin] Luther, [John] Calvin, [Philip] Melancthon, [Martin] Bucer, [Justin] Martyr, and many others, stood up against all the rest of the world; they preached and prayed and wrote; and nations agreed one after another to cast off the yoke of popery, and to embrace the doctrine of the gospel. In England, episcopal tyranny succeeded popish cruelty, which, in the year 1620, obliged many pious people to leave their native land and settle in America; these were followed by others in 1629, who laid the foundations of several gospel churches, which have increased amazingly since that time, and the Redeemer has fixed His throne in that country, where but a little time ago, Satan had universal dominion.

In 1632, Mr. John Elliot, of New England, a very pious and zealous minister, began to preach to the Indians, among whom he had great success...About the year 1743, Mr. David Brainerd was sent as a missionary to some more Indians, where he preached, and prayed, and after some time an extraordinary work of conversion was underway...In 1706, the king of Denmark sent a Mr. [Bartholomaüs] Ziegenbalg, and some others to Tranquebar, on the Coromandel coast in the East Indies, who were useful to the natives, so that many of the heathens were turned to the Lord. The Dutch East India Company likewise having extended their commerce, built the city of Batavia, and a church was opened there...The work has decayed in some places, but they now have churches in Ceylon, Sumatra, Java, Amboyna, and some other of the Spice Islands and at the Cape of Good Hope in Africa...

What a heaven will it be to see the many myriads of poor heathens, of Britons amongst the rest, who by their labors have been brought to the knowledge of God. Surely a crown of rejoicing like this is worth aspiring to. Surely it is worthwhile to lay ourselves out with all our might in promoting the cause and kingdom of Christ.

DAY 29
The Missionary Age: Half-Century Discourse: Part 1 of 3
by Rufus Anderson
(Excerpted from *The Missionary Age: a Half-Century Discourse*, published by
T. R. Marvin, Boston, Massachusetts in 1851)

When the fullness of time was come, God sent His Son.
Galatians 4:4

At the opening of the present century [1800's], a few missions [bases
of operations in foreign cultures], mostly of recent origin, might be
seen faintly twinkling out from the depths of pagan darkness. But
they were feebly sustained, had gained no stronghold on the heathen
world, and awakened no general interest among the churches. Never
did any age, not even the apostolic, behold such a system of
missions as we are now permitted to see. They are not universal up
to now, for some portions of the world are as yet scarcely accessible.
But the Christian traveler would find them on nearly all the more
important points along two thousand miles of the African coast; in
nearly every important center of influence in Western Asia; on the
upper waters of the Indus River [India]; along the Ganges River
[India]; around nearly the whole shoreline of India, and over nearly
the length and breadth of its great peninsula. He would find them in
Ceylon [Sri Lanka], in Assam [northeast India], in Siam [Thailand],
in the Indian Archipelago [Malaysia and Indonesia], and in the five
chief ports of the Chinese empire…Christian missions already
provide a more effective and better protection to the sailor in that
"Island World," than could be furnished by all the navies of
Christendom. And along the great rivers of our western wilds, after
crossing the Rocky Mountains, how often would the traveler be
gladdened at evening by the songs of Zion, when fearing he should
hear the war-cry of the savage!

Though all this is but the beginning of the enterprise for the world's conversion (and it is nothing more), yet how great is that beginning!—how wide!—in how many places!—how extended over the earth! You find the messengers of the cross both in the burning and temperate zones, in every region; encountering every form of barbarism, every language, every religion; and laboring—with equal cheerfulness—in every part of the unevangelized world. Nor are these missionaries laboring in vain. Theirs, through God's blessing, is one of the most successful great enterprises that was ever undertaken by man. Look at the Sandwich Islands [Hawaii]. Look at the long line of island-groups in the South Pacific. Look at New Zealand.

Behold, Cherokee and Choctaw nations, the "wild Indian" both civilized and Christianized. Behold in Western Asia, the two religious reformations now in progress, among the Armenians and the Nestorians [Persia]. Behold in Africa, West and South, the many thousands gathered into churches. Behold the increasing number of Christian villages in India...Behold the multitude of schools, the seminaries, the native preachers, the printing establishments. Behold the hundred and twenty languages of the pagan world lately transformed into writing, and now beginning to be enriched with the Scriptures, and with schoolbooks and religious tracts. Behold at least a thousand churches, with two or three hundred thousand members, enjoying the services of some fifteen hundred foreign missionaries and thousands of native Christian helpers...Behold nearly forty million Scriptures issued by Bible societies—a greater number than ever before since the Law was given on Mount Sinai; and billions of tracts and religious books issued by Tract and Sunday-school societies. I might also speak of the stimulus that has thus been given to our religious education, to our religious literature...to our churches and religious bodies, and to all of our evangelical denominations. I might show how this vastly extended generous enterprise has raised the character of the Christian Church, and secured for it an attention among people that it never had before...

DAY 30
The Missionary Age: Half-Century Discourse: Part 2 of 3
by Rufus Anderson
(Excerpted from *The Missionary Age: a Half-Century Discourse*, published by
T. R. Marvin, Boston, Massachusetts in 1851)

When the fullness of time was come, God sent His Son.
Galatians 4:4

Now how do you account for all this? What does it mean? Why within the memory of many now living has the world been in this way strangely opened and made accessible, as by a stupendous miracle? And why has such a vast systematic organization grown up as in a day, of associations at home and missions abroad, with the specific and declared purpose of declaring the gospel to every creature? Was there ever such a thing before? Why has the great and blessed God crowded so many such stupendous results into our day?

I am unable to answer these inquiries, except on the idea that the "fullness of time" has actually come for the predicted publication and spread of the gospel through the world. I am sure that they cannot be answered on any other thought. There never has been an age like the present. Never did churches, or individual Christians, or any person with the gospel in their hands, stand in such a relation to the heathen world as we do now. Not only is that world accessible, but it even lies on our very borders. We cannot sympathize with Richard Baxter [theologian in the 17th-century], in his almost despairing hope that the time might come when the gospel should have access to the Orient; for with us, hope has given place to certainty, and every man, woman and child may now operate, with the greatest ease, upon the most distant nations. People sometimes complain of the frequency and urgency of the calls that are made on their religious goodwill. But do they not see that the most urgent of these calls result necessarily from the character which God has stamped on our age, and from the relation in which we stand to the surrounding world? Our ancestors of the last century had no such calls upon them, as we have from nations beyond the bounds of Christendom; and they had not, because those nations were then comparatively unknown or unapproachable. But God has been pleased, in our day, to lift the shroud of death from off the heathen world, and to bring the world near, and to fill our eyes with the sight and our ears with the cry of their distress. He has leveled the mountains and bridged the oceans, which separated the unenlightened nations from us, and has made for us highways to every land.

He says to us, "Go"—with an emphasis and a meaning such as this command never had to ministers and Christians in former ages. If we could take the wings of the morning, and fly millions of miles beyond our globe, we could by no means escape from the responsibility that has come upon us; for we know our duty, and we can never be as though we had not known it. We would be held and treated, wherever found by ministering angels, as deserters from the army of the Lord of hosts.

God's Word and Spirit and Providence now all agree in the command to carry the gospel to all the nations; and if we refuse, the blood of perishing nations will cry against us. This is the age for the work, and we are the people to do it. Christ will give us no release from this warfare. It is not logical that we shall be saved in neglecting this work because our predecessors were. Our circumstances differ wholly from theirs. Western Asia, India, China were shut to them, but are open to us. Neither had God been inclined to teach them, as He has us, to associate and combine their strength and act in masses for the accomplishment of great religious enterprises.

DAY 31
The Missionary Age: Half-Century Discourse: Part 3 of 3
by Rufus Anderson

(Excerpted from *The Missionary Age: a Half-Century Discourse*, published by
T. R. Marvin, Boston, Massachusetts in 1851)

When the fullness of time was come, God sent His Son.
Galatians 4:4

Truly, it is no fleeting opinion, nor mere popular sentiment, accidentally arisen and liable to pass away, that has put out and sustains the missionary work. It is the onward, almost overwhelming progress of God's gracious providence. As long as there is liberty of thought, speech and action, a free press, an advancing civilization, and an unshackled, universal commerce, we may be sure that the motives to perform the missionary work will continue to increase in their multiplied power upon the hearts, consciences and conduct of the Christian Church...

These mighty beginnings of the past half-century will have glorious developments in the half-century to come; and the children will have far more to do and will do far more than their ancestors did or believed that they could do.

The idea that the ability of the churches to give is already fully accomplished comes from a profound ignorance of the statistics of our religious charities. Nearly one-half of the three million professed evangelical church members in our country are believed yet to give anything at all for missions—foreign or domestic. Nearly a third, even in New England, are believed to give nothing; and very many, even in our own denomination, contribute not more than half a dollar a year for propagating the gospel; which is at the rate of twenty-five dollars in half a century! Or, if twice this sum, it would be but fifty dollars during a long, long lifetime! And for the purpose that brought the Son of God on His mission from Heaven to earth! Are these faithful stewards? Will they hear the heaven-creating words, "Well done!" addressed to them on the great day, by the Judge on the throne?

I am not pleading especially for any one missionary society, nor for any one class of missions, nor for the millions of any one nation or continent. I stand on higher, broader ground. I am pleading for the general cause of missions and of the gospel. I am pleading for the world in view of the length, breadth, depth, and height of the love of Christ, and of our obligations to Him. Is this a work we may do, or may not do? Is it to be counted among mere human enterprises? Can we neglect it, and think calmly of our neglect in our dying day?

Let us understand the full influence of our duty. Let us awaken to its great reality. Nothing is more truly binding upon us than the obligation to impart the gospel to those whom we can reach and who will perish if they do not receive it. That surely is the most destructive immorality which withholds from immortal people the only gospel of salvation. The most wicked infidelity is surely that which does not care for a world perishing in sin. And that must be the most high-handed disregard of Heaven's authority, and must reflect the most dishonor upon the Son of God which refuses, in the face of His most explicit command, to declare His gospel to every creature.

Let us remember that He who requires this is our God, in whose hands are our possessions, our lives, and our immortal souls, and that our opportunities are rushing by us and fast passing away forever!

DAY 32
Excerpts from the Letters of General C. G. "Chinese" Gordon:
(Excerpted from *Letters of General C. G. Gordon*, by M. A. Gordon, published by Macmillan and Company, London in 1897)

There is not the least doubt that there is an immense virgin field for an apostle in these countries among the black tribes. They are virgin to my belief, and the apostle would have nothing to contend with like the fanaticism of the Arabs. But where will you find an apostle? I will explain what I mean by the term. He or she must be a person who has died entirely to the world; who has no ties of any sort; who longs for death when it may please God to do so; who can bear the intense dullness of these countries; who seeks for few letters; and who can bear the thought of dying deserted. Now there are few, very, very few people who can accept this post. But no half-measures will do…A person must give up *everything*, understand *everything, everything*, to do anything for Christ here. No half nor three-quarter measures will do. And yet, what a field!...One must believe that God is the absolute Ruler of all events, good or bad. He directs the one and permits the other, but governs both for His glory. They must believe that God does even now work with His Spirit, and that He can, without words, make people realize divine truths…To tell you plainly, I think the price God asks of a person who comes out to live among the tribes is too great for anyone to pay. I know none, no, not one, who could pay it…Perhaps I may have exaggerated the price God requires; but I think not…

I would mention that the life a person lives is the one which the blacks would understand better than a person's words. All people can read a person's life, and they will judge their religion by their life…The first thing which has to be done is to open and facilitate communication with their countries. Next, to let the natives mix with more civilized races, so as to acquire their language, their own native tongue being so poor as not to contain more than 300 words.

Do you understand that, with a language of 300 words, any explanation, even of secular affairs, must be difficult, and how much more so must be the explanation of religious truths like the Atonement, which few of us are given to properly understand?...I believe sincerely that a person, spiritually dead to the world and giving one's self as a sacrifice in these countries, could, by consistent holy walk and acts, imprint higher thoughts in the population they lived among. One's life would be the preaching; but who would have the faith to undergo this exile?...Nations are as individuals in some respects. Nations almost invariably have acquired some degree of civilization before Christianity has taken root. In our own land the Roman civilization prepared the way for the gospel...

With the exception of the inland mission in China, our own and foreign missions confine their efforts to the ports, where there is much more society and comfort for their apostles than being exiled in the interior. The Roman Catholics in China were certainly far more self-sacrificing. I went out with some twenty young [Catholic] men who definitely stated that they went out never to return, and said goodbye to their friends as if they were going to their execution. I never have seen or heard of any Protestant missionary being so compelled. Was not their action more Christ-like than those of our persuasion who go out to the ports with £300 a year for a couple or for four years, and whose bread is sure, while these Roman Catholic students went and lived as they could among the native Chinese? Why does the Catholic Church thrive with so many errors in it? It is because of these godly men in her who live Christ's life, and who, like as Zoar was spared for Lot's sake, bring a blessing on the whole community. For self-devotion, for self-denial, the Roman Catholic Church is in advance of our present day Protestantism. What is it if you know the sound truths and do not act up to them? Actions speak loudly and are read by all; words are as the breath of man.

DAY 33
Missionary Heroes in Africa: Part 1 of 3
by Robert Needham Cust

(Excerpted from *The Gospel Message: Christian Missions to Non-Christian Races and Peoples*, published by Luzac & Company, London, England 1896)

We read often in secular books, and too often in missionary biographies, how our Heavenly Father is supposed on some occasions to have graciously intervened to save the life of one of His poor children: in Roman Catholic accounts this benevolent interference is attributed to the Virgin Mary or St. Theresa. Not a sparrow indeed falls without His command; but if such interference is presumed when a good person's life is saved, how shall we account for the absence of this Providential care when a good person is cruelly killed or cut off by premature disease? But this is a narrow view of God's Providence. His ways are not our ways. He has chosen His servants for particular service: some to honor; some to dishonor. Some are selected to live and work, to others is given the special grace to die nobly and set a glorious example. Deaths are required as well as lives to complete the picture of the New Life. Some may follow the steps of our Lord in a life of generosity and mercy; to others is granted the sweeter destiny of filling up that which is lacking in His sufferings. And in the last struggle how by grace they have been sustained, doing nothing common or insignificant in the last memorable scene of their earthly passion, but sealing their faith by their manner of meeting death!

I quote a noble passage from the Chronicle of the London Missionary Society:

> It is no unimportant thing to be a link in God's chain of causes, to have a mission from God to discharge in the world, however low the office and the duty may be. It is better to recognize this Mission, and diligently to cultivate

qualifications for it, and still better persistently and faithfully, and always for God, to strive to fill the place and do the work of this Divine commission.

Hear some of the dying words of these soldiers of Christ. In the hour of death all things are terribly real. There is no room for deception or false enthusiasm then. I have selected these words without distinction of country or denomination, but their number might be multiplied indefinitely.

Arrhenius, the Swede, had only a few months of labor in the Galla country [a people in East Africa] after years of preparation for his duties: his last words were: "Jesus, help me! Jesus, help me! Amen." Praetorius, the Swiss, was sent out for a few months' inspection of the missions on the Gold Coast: he called upon me on his way out, and promised to call again on his return; but after a few weeks in Africa he fell. His last words were: "Is it true that I am going home today?"

Of all the smaller English [missionary] associations, Harley House-Bow was conspicuous for its overflowing of zeal and life and promise, and of all its agents, McCall was the brightest; but he was struck down in mid-work. His last words were recorded by a stranger who visited him on his solitary deathbed. Let each one of us lay them to our hearts: "Lord, I gave myself, body, mind, and soul, to Thee. I consecrated my whole life and being to Thy service, and now, if it please Thee to take myself, instead of the work, which I would do for Thee, what is that to me? Thy will be done!" He had hoped that his destined course might have been among the brave and strong, to toil with high purpose for the welfare of the African; but God had chosen another role for him, and as a true Christian, he recognized that God had chosen it well and no weak complaints escaped the lips of one who was ready to live or ready to die...

DAY 34
Missionary Heroes in Africa: Part 2 of 3
by Robert Needham Cust

(Excerpted from *The Gospel Message: Christian Missions to Non-Christian Races and Peoples*, published by Luzac & Company, London, England 1896)

Golaz, of the French Mission to Senegambia [West Africa], as well as his young wife, died within the year after their arrival: his farewell words were: "Do not be discouraged if the first laborers fall in the field. Their graves will mark the way for their successors, who will march past them with great strides."

Pinkerton, of the American Mission in Zululand [South Africa], was ordered to lead a new Mission into Umzila's Kingdom: he took his wife and children to North America, and returned joyfully to his task. He met with many obstacles and rejections, but at length found himself well on the road. His last written lines were to his wife: "The future will bring its needed light, and work, and solace. My thoughts turn sadly to you and our children. All well. We go right on." It was to him, indeed, all well, for in a few days he breathed his last sigh alone in the African jungle: he had gone right on into Glory. On the other side of Africa, Bagster, of the same mission, had been sent to found a mission among the A-Mbandu: a few months before his death he had proposed to write on "The Missionary's Joys." In the last page of his journal we find: "We hear His voice of cheer: Go forward: one man of you shall chase ten thousand: the Lord your God has promised you the good land, which He has given to you: most joyous is the service of our King!"

[George] Thomson, of the Baptist Mission in the Kamerun [Cameroon] country (that famous mission which during 1885-86 was uprooted and destroyed by the late German Emperor), a few weeks before his death in December, 1884, unconscious of the ruin which was soon to come upon the scene of his labors, on his chapels, and his mission-schools, wrote as follows:

> I am sustained and upheld amid many and heavy anxieties by the growing conviction that the dear Master is, in His great condescension, using me here for the settlement of many difficulties; and I look forward to the future with more hope than I have known for years. I believe that the work here will soon assume a better and brighter aspect, and my heart glows within me, as by faith I see the time. Oh for more and more of grace to cast all our burdens upon the Divine burden-bearer! Our hope and trust are in Him alone!

With such people (and these few are but types of many) Africa and the whole world can be conquered. Such deaths are great victories. Such words tell us that some portion of us is immortal. These confessors saw the promises afar off, and were persuaded by them, confessing that they were strangers and pilgrims, and desiring a better country, that is, a Heavenly one...

The last journal of [James] Hannington (who was present when I read this address in 1888) brings this point of view vividly before me. I can see that faithful Christian in the midst of his sad environment, oppressed with anxiety for the future of the work to which he had dedicated himself, still sustained by the daily reading of, and meditation upon, the Book of Psalms. We find in these pages, so wonderfully preserved, no religious murmuring, no cries for vengeance, no appeal to the arm of the flesh. Still, as he lay tossing on his unsavory heap of straw, before his feverish eyes, during those sad days and weary nights, no doubt rose the vision of the peaceful home, the pleasing duties, the loved companion, the little children, whom he had voluntarily left, obeying the call to serve his Master; and not in vain, for a still voice would whisper to him: "It is the Lord's will: obedience is of the essence of true courage, and true Love. The battles of the Heavenly King are fought in suffering as well as doing, and in dishonor, in prison...as truly as in the Mission Chapel, the Mission School, and the center of a Christian village."

DAY 35
Missionary Heroes in Africa: Part 3 of 3
by Robert Needham Cust
(Excerpted from *The Gospel Message: Christian Missions to Non-Christian Races and Peoples*, published by Luzac & Company, London, England 1896)

The following were the dying words of a Missionary in 1890: his last words, uttered with great difficulty, were: "I—have—made—it—my—purpose—through—life—to—follow—Christ."

At the age of seventy-four, I may humbly express a wish to die with these words on my lips. We seem at this period of the history of our missionary churches to be living over again the trials and persecutions of the early Christians in the second century. Do we not seem to hear the echo of the words of the Virgin-Saint [Joan of Arc], who at Aries in France was slowly let down feet-forward into a vessel of boiling oil, because she refused to deny her Master? "Jesus Christ, help me! Praise be to Thee! Lord Jesus, grant me patience! I suffer for Thy name's sake: I suffer for a little time only: I suffer of my own accord. Jesus, let me never be confounded! take me! take me!"

Time would fail me to tell of Schlenker, and Reichardt, and Schon; of Goldie and Edgerley; of Casalis, Mabille, and Coillard, of James Stewart of Lovedale, and his namesake on the Nyasa [South Africa]; of Grant and Wilson; of Ramseyer and Christaller; of Mackenzie, the bishop, who died on the River Shire [Malawi]; of Steere, the bishop, who sealed up the translation of the last chapter of Isaiah ready for the printer, and then fell asleep at Zanzibar [Tanzania]; of Parker, the bishop, wise and gentle, holy and self-restrained, who was called to his rest on the shores of Victoria Nyanza [Lake Victoria]; of Hill, the bishop, whom the Lord called to Himself on the day of his landing in Lagos to take up his duties; of dear Maples, the Bishop, who was drowned in Lake Nyasa [South Africa]; of Mackay, who for ten years held the fort at Uganda, and died at his post; of Wakefield and New; of Stern and Mayer; of Southon, who died at U-Rambo [Tanzania]; of Mullens, who could not hold himself back from the fight, and who sleeps in U-Sagara [Tanzania]; of many a gentle woman's grave, for women have never been found lacking to share the honor and the danger of the Cross.

I have seen and known so many of them. A few weeks before we were holding sweet conversation, and then the tidings of the death of one of them came floating back by letter or telegram. They had indeed all gone into a far country, and to me they all seem to be there still. And when I am musing about Africa, or studying some point connected with that country, and I look up from my paper to my African library, the forms of departed friends seem to enter at the open door, and I seem to see their faces again, and want to ask them their opinion. Young Riviere, a Jesuit priest, who had been turned out of Algeria and had taken refuge in North Wales, used to correspond with me about Africa. One day he called upon me in London and told me that he had received his orders to start at once to the Zambesi [Zambia/Zimbabwe] mission-field, to take the place of a dead colleague. He promised to write to me from Tete, and to clear up many questions for me; but he never reached his destination, for he sank under his first attack of fever at the mouth of the Zambesi. Differing as I do from the Church of Rome in their dogma and practice, and detail of their system, I can still recognize and thank God for the zeal, and love of souls, and total surrender of self which distinguish her missionaries. Oh, when they are such, I wish that they were ours!

...I quote Bishop Westcott's words: "The clergy have their functions, but the bearing abroad of the message of the gospel belongs to the believer as believer, whether laity, or ordained."...We owe this debt to those who have gone before, that they should not have died in vain. The missionary is indeed the most glorious outcome of the nineteenth century; the honest, God-fearing man or woman in the darkest corner of the earth, where he or she is most wanted, to represent the highest type of Christian patience and morality.

DAY 36
Address to Females in America, Relative to the Situation of Heathen Females in the East: Part 1 of 2
by Mrs. Adoniram (Ann Hasseltine) Judson

(Excerpted from *Memoir of Mrs. Ann H. Judson*, published by Wightman and Cramp, London, England in 1829)

In the land of my birth, rendered doubly dear from the long-held thought of never again beholding it; in the country favored by Heaven above most others, it is with uncommon sensations I address my sisters and female friends on this most interesting subject. Favored as we are from infancy with instruction of every kind, used as we are to view the female mind in its proper state, and accustomed as we are to feel the happy effects of female influence, our thoughts would turn away from the melancholy subject of female degradation, of female wretchedness. But will our feelings of pity and compassion, will those feelings which alone render the female character lovely, allow us to turn away to dismiss the subject altogether, without making an effort to rescue, to save? No! I think I hear your united voices echo the reply: "Our efforts shall be joined with yours. Show us the situation of our sisters on the other side of the world, and though the disgusting picture might break our hearts, it will fill us with gratitude to Him who has made us different, and excite us to stronger exertions in their behalf." Listen, then, to my tale of woe!

In Bengal and India, the females in the higher classes are excluded from the society of men. At the age of two or three years, they are married by their parents to children of their own rank in society. On these occasions all the parade and splendor possible are exhibited; they are then conducted back to their father's home, not to be educated, not to prepare for the performance of the duties compulsory of wives and mothers, but to drag out the usual period allotted, in lifeless idleness, in mental inactivity. At the age of thirteen, fourteen, or fifteen, they are demanded by their husbands, to whose home they are moved, where again confinement is their fate. No social interaction is allowed to cheer their gloomy hours; nor do they have the consolation of feeling that they are viewed, even by their husbands, as companions. Far from receiving those delicate attentions which make the conjugal state happy, and which distinguish civilized from heathen nations, the wife receives the label of "my servant" or "my dog," and is allowed to partake of what her lordly husband is pleased to give at the conclusion of his meal!

In this secluded, degraded situation, females in India receive no instruction; consequently, they are wholly uninformed about an eternal state. No wonder mothers consider female existence a curse; therefore they desire to destroy their female offspring and burn themselves with the bodies of their deceased husbands. This last circumstance might imply some attachment, were it not a well-known fact that the disgrace of a woman who refuses to burn with the corpse of her husband is such that her nearest relations would refuse her a morsel of rice to prevent her starvation. Thus the females of Bengal are utterly deprived of all enjoyment, both here and hereafter. Such is their life and their death, and here the scene is closed to mortal view! But they are pleasant, say some, and lacking those violent passions which are exhibited among females in our own country. My beloved friends, be not deceived. Whoever heard that ignorance was favorable to the culture of pleasant feelings? Their minds are so weak that we might hope to find at least an absence of vicious feelings. But facts prove the contrary. Whenever an opportunity for exhibiting the destructive passions of the soul occurs, human nature never made a more vigorous effort to reveal this odious deformity than has been observed in these secluded females.

DAY 37
Address to Females in America, Relative to the Situation of Heathen Females in the East: Part 2 of 2
by Mrs. Adoniram (Ann Hasseltine) Judson
(Excerpted from *Memoir of Mrs. Ann H. Judson*, published by Wightman and Cramp, London, England in 1829)

But let us turn our eyes from the present picture to one not less heart-rending, but where hope may have a greater influence to brighten and to cheer. The females in the Burmese Empire (containing a population far exceeding the United States of America), are not like the females in Bengal, secluded from all society. In this respect they are on an equality with ourselves. Wives are allowed the privilege of eating with their husbands. They engage in domestic concerns, and thus, in some respects, the Burmese females deserve our particular sympathy and attention. But they enjoy little of the confidence or affection of their husbands, and to be born a female is universally considered a special misfortune. The wife and grown daughters are considered by the husband and father as much the subjects of discipline, as younger children; hence it is a common thing for females of every age and description to suffer under the tyrannical rod of those who should be their protectors.

Burma, also, like her sister nations, allows the female mind to remain in its uneducated state, without an effort to show how much more highly she has been favored. The females of this country are lively, inquisitive, strong, and energetic, open to friendship...and possess minds naturally capable of growing to the highest state of cultivation and refinement. But they are taught nothing that has a tendency to cherish these best native feelings of the heart! That they possess strong energetic minds is evident from their mode of conversing, and from their inquisitiveness.

It may be interesting to mention a particular display of mental energy as exhibited in the early inquiries of Mah Men-la. At some time prior to our arrival in Rangoon, her active mind was led to inquire about the origin of all things. If Buddha was deity, who created all that her eyes beheld? She inquired of this person and that, visited all the teachers within the circle of her acquaintance, but none was able to give her satisfactory information on the subject. Her anxiety increased to such a degree that her own family feared she would be deranged. She finally resolved to learn to read so that she might be able to gain the desired information from their sacred books. Her husband, willing to gratify her curiosity in this respect, taught her to read himself. After having acquired what very few Burmese females are allowed to acquire, she studied the sacred books, which left her mind in the same inquisitive state as when she commenced. For ten years she had continued her inquiries, when, one day, a neighbor brought in a tract written by Mr. Judson, from which she derived her first ideas of an eternal God. Her next difficulty arose from her being ignorant of the residence of the author of the tract, and it was not until after the erection of the zayat [shelter for travelers] that this difficulty was removed. By her inquiries about the Christian religion, she demonstrated a mind, which, had it been early and properly cultivated, would hardly have been surpassed by females in our own country. And I am happy to add that she not only became rationally…convinced of the truths of the gospel, but was, I trust, taught to feel their power on her heart, by the influence of the Holy Spirit, embraced them, has become a compliment to her profession, and her daily walk and conversation would shame many professors of religion in Christian countries.

Shall we, my beloved friends, allow minds like these to lie dormant, to wither in ignorance and delusion, to grope their way to eternal ruin, without an effort on our part to raise, to refine, to elevate, and to point to that Savior who has died equally for them as for us?

DAY 38
The Message in the Tongues of Men: Part 1 of 5
by William Owen Carver
(Excerpted from *The Bible a Missionary Message*, published by Fleming H. Revell Company, New York, New York in 1921)

And how is it that we hear, each of us in his own native language?
Acts 2:8

***

A Necessary Element in Expanding Christianity
This work of translating the Bible message belongs to the periods when Christians have been reading and studying its words, and have been stirred by the missionary inspiration, an inspiration which an understanding from reading the Bible always arouses.

Up to the beginning of the modern missionary period [late 1700's], it had been put into twenty-eight languages. Bible translation and missionary activity go together. Bible translation is a method of missions. It is one of the most important and successful of all methods and is absolutely necessary to the permanent establishment of a vigorous, conquering Christianity in any part of the world. Jesus and His apostles used the common speech of their day; they spoke also in the Greek language, which had been brought into Palestine, as it had gone into all the ancient world and had become the common international speech of humankind in that day. Not only did they speak in the languages common to the people of their day, as a rule they quoted their scriptures, our Old Testament, not in its original but now antiquated Hebrew form, but in its Greek translation. This translation could be read by most intelligent Jews in Palestine, was read by most Jews outside Palestine, and was the only form in which non-Jews read it.

Thus in spirit and in practice, Jesus and the apostles are squarely against any notion of a "sacred language" in which God's message is hidden from others. If we follow their example we shall seek to have all people hearing and reading "in their own tongues the mighty works of God" (Acts 2:11). Does not the gift of tongues on the day of Pentecost mean that the Holy Spirit intends for us to give God's message to all people in their own languages? All the people in Jerusalem at that time could understand either Aramaic or Greek; but the Spirit of Jesus caused the people from all fourteen regions to hear in the tongue native to each one.

Muslims have bitterly opposed all translation of their Qu'ran and, until quite recently, have prohibited it and done all that is possible to prevent it. They have no message in it that will tolerate translation. In any but the Arabic language its lack of spiritual power and appeal are made evident.

Roman Catholics have regarded Latin as the holy language of our Scriptures and have not encouraged their being put into the languages of the people. They have discouraged private reading of the Bible even where the people knew its language, resulting in moral stagnation and hindered religious development. It is at this point, more seriously than at any other, that their missions have failed. They do not give their converts the Word of God, and they never plant a pure Christianity that can set their converts on the way to become a vigorous, progressive, ethical force in the life of the people. Even the missionaries themselves do not have full knowledge nor any adequate appreciation of the Bible. The Jesuit missions to the Indians of the valleys of the St. Lawrence and the Mississippi and of the Middle West constitute one of the finest chapters of heroic devotion and personal sacrifice for the sake of the heathen. Yet they left no abiding influence because they failed to deliver God's message in the languages of the Indians.

DAY 39
The Message in the Tongues of Men: Part 2 of 5
by William Owen Carver
(Excerpted from *The Bible a Missionary Message*, published by Fleming H. Revell Company, New York, New York in 1921)

And how is it that we hear, each of us in his own native language?
Acts 2:8

John Elliot, in Massachusetts, succeeded in building Christian Indian towns and changing the whole idea and habits of the life of the Mohicans; and a great factor in his success was his translation of the Bible into their language, the first translation (1661-1663) into any Indian tongue. That white men destroyed these Christian villages is a tragic illustration of how we need the religion of Christ translated also into terms of political and social relations and conduct.

Sketch of the History of Translation
In the spread of Christianity in the early centuries, for a thousand years in fact, it was the custom to carry the Bible into the lands where Christianity went. This was especially true for the first five centuries. Before this, the Old Testament, in its Greek translation, had played a large part in preparing for the coming of Christ and for the mission of His gospel in the world. It was in the third century B.C., and in Alexandria [Egypt], that this translation was produced. It is called the Septuagint, because of the tradition that seventy Jewish scholars worked at the task of producing it. That enlightened King, the great library builder of Alexandria, Ptolemy Philadelphus, is said to have desired it for his growing collections there. But its Hebrew form would have met that need unless it was to be read.

The ever-growing multitudes of Jews in that city and in all other cities of the Greek-speaking world were less and less able to read their Bible in its Hebrew form, and found it far easier to get the words of their God in the newer form. And the beauty and power of the message it carried made this Greek Old Testament a book sought by eager Gentile souls in all the Greco-Roman world. And so it had a great missionary career even before Christ had come. In nearly every city "God-fearing" heathen men and women read this Septuagint and worshipped, as they might, the God whose messages it brought them. When the missionaries of Christ went out with this story, they found these Bible readers ready to accept the Lord's Christ and they became charter members of many a Christian church in the first century. They were an element of great strength in the growing churches.

Before the end of the first century, translations for missionary purposes had begun. By the third century, besides its original Greek, the New Testament, and in part also the Old Testament, were read in the Syriac, Armenian, Coptic, Ethiopian and Latin languages and cultures. The evidence is more than abundant that Bible reading in the native tongues was the common practice of Christians in the various lands. Special provision was made for such reading by the new converts and by those seeking admission into the churches. [Bishop] Cyprian taught that it was of the highest importance to read God's word, because "In prayer we speak to God, but in reading the Scriptures He speaks to us."

[Adolf von] Harnack has produced the evidence that from their infancy children were taught the Bible, even by means of their "ivory letter-blocks." "The children daily hear the Scriptures read and learn passages of them by heart; a Bible was not only in the home: the Bible was the principal textbook of education; the chief aim in the whole training of a child was that they should be taught to understand the Bible." Such use of the Bible not only made missions successful but stimulated the missionary activity of those early Christians until they still surprise and shame our modern Christians. Their Bible sent them out with the glorious message to the ends of the earth.

DAY 40
The Message in the Tongues of Men: Part 3 of 5
by William Owen Carver
(Excerpted from *The Bible a Missionary Message*, published by Fleming H. Revell
Company, New York, New York in 1921)

And how is it that we hear, each of us in his own native language?
Acts 2:8

In the fourth century, there were two notable versions. Jerome made
a new version in Latin that became the sacred, standard Bible of the
Roman Church. It is known as "the Vulgate," a name that ought
forever to shame the Church that seeks to retain the Word of God
in a form long since outgrown. *Vulgus* means "the crowd," "the
masses." The Vulgate was the Bible for the people, the common
person. When language changed with the development of the
people, the language of the Bible should have been changed so as to
keep it in the mouths and minds of common folk. Yet we still have
thousands upon thousands of Protestants and Baptists who think a
translation into the English of three hundred years ago is somehow
more truly the Word of God than a translation into the terms of our
English of the twentieth century.

Ulfilas was the great missionary to the Goths, for whose sakes he
left Constantinople and crossed the Danube to give these wild
barbarians the gospel of the grace of God. He invented an alphabet
in order that he might put the Word of God in the language of this
people. By this he laid the foundation not only for their
Christianization but for Germanic culture as well. It is of interest
that he omitted from his version of the Old Testament the war
histories of Israel because he felt that these Goths were too warlike
and he thought they would misunderstand and think God's approval
sanctioned their bloody career. This Bible became the chief treasure
of these migratory hordes, its manuscript copies being carried with

them into Spain and Africa and to Rome. And the influence of this Bible translation modified the impact and influence of these heathen on the civilization and religion of the Roman world.

In the Rise and Growth of Protestantism

Protestantism founded itself on the Bible. In Germany and in England, the Bible in the language of the people became the greatest factor in enlightenment and progress. In both lands it became the greatest classic of their literature and the most persuasive, the most sanctifying, the most inspiring influence in literature, in political progress, in religious reformation and growth. Literally hundreds of volumes in Europe and America have drawn their titles from the Bible, have built their characters on Biblical material, have shaped their plots and plans from Biblical teaching. And our literatures in all Christian lands are filled with the language and the ideas of which the Bible is an inexhaustible source.

***

In the Modern Missionary Era

In the various missionary lands, more than a hundred and fifty mission presses produce Bibles, Testaments, Gospels and other portions of the Scriptures, tracts, Sunday school literature, and other periodicals.

In very great measure these publishing interests are able to meet their expenses from the sales and from gifts from natives who appreciate the great service they render, when once they have become established in their work of blessing and had time to produce a reading public.

***

DAY 41
The Message in the Tongues of Men: Part 4 of 5
by William Owen Carver
(Excerpted from *The Bible a Missionary Message*, published by Fleming H. Revell
Company, New York, New York in 1921)

And how is it that we hear, each of us in his own native language?
Acts 2:8

In Closed Lands
When the missionaries could not go into closed lands and labor in person, they have used the printed Bible to carry God's message and to prepare a way for the spoken word to follow later. The pioneer of missions in China, Robert Morrison, after twenty-seven years of fervent toil, died six years before his successors were permitted to take up residence in the five Chinese cities first opened to foreign residence. He and his co-laborers, Milne, Medhurst and others, had to labor outside among emigrants. Meantime, with wonderful gifts and grace, he put the Bible message into Chinese and his first native helper, Liang Afah, could carry it in and get it into the hands of some of his people. The noble and original Dr. [Karl] Gutzlaff not only did splendid work of translation but boldly distributed his tracts and Gospels from a houseboat in which he "invaded" the Chinese coastland waterways.

Morrison stood at the gates and produced a dictionary and a grammar to go along with his Bible, and so provided the materials for carrying the gospel to China's heathen when it should finally unlock the doors. In similar ways the Word of God on printed page went before the missionaries in Japan and Korea, and for many years told its story in "the Forbidden Land" of Tibet before any messenger was permitted to proclaim salvation there.

Muslims have been most inaccessible to direct missionary approach.

Wherever the political control has been in Muslim hands, definite efforts to win converts from "the Faith" were absolutely prohibited. The first missionaries to Turkish territory, a hundred years ago now, took with them a printing press, at first operating it on British territory beyond the reach of Turkish hands. Besides this source of silent, subtle "invasion," the missionaries found that Christian education could not be barred even from Turkey, as long as active propaganda among Muslim students was omitted. With divinely imparted patience and wisdom, these men and women sowed the good seed of the Word and now the fruits are justifying their faith with the hope of rich harvests soon to follow.

Taking advantage of the Muslim reverence for the "holy" Arabic of the original Qu'ran, which educated Muslims read the world over, our Testament and Bible in various attractive editions have been put into the hands of very many, while also they have been translated into Turkish and other languages spoken by sections of the two hundred million followers of the Prophet. An illustration of what this sort of evangelism may be accomplishing is found in the story of a Muslim found reading the New Testament. On being asked why he was reading that book, he replied: "Ah, there is nothing that scours the sin out of my heart like this."

It is no wonder the Bible is the world's book in ever-increasing measure. It is not easy to grasp the vast demand for it. No other book is at all to be compared with it. Dickens is the most popular writer in all secular literature. From the first until now it is estimated that twenty-five million copies of all his works combined have been sold. In a single year, of the whole and of parts, thirty-five million copies of God's Word were distributed among the people.

***

DAY 42
The Message in the Tongues of Men: Part 5 of 5
by William Owen Carver
(Excerpted from *The Bible a Missionary Message*, published by Fleming H. Revell
Company, New York, New York in 1921)

And how is it that we hear, each of us in his own native language?
Acts 2:8

William Carey, "Father of the Modern Missionary Enterprise," translated the Scriptures into a score of languages and edited others until, in whole or in part, he set the Bible free in thirty-six languages in India. And early on he set up a printing plant for their circulation. One of the stories of mingled romance and heroism is that of [Adoniram] Judson's Burmese Bible, the manuscript of which was first preserved by his faithful wife, concealed in his pillow during part of his terrible prison sufferings, thrown out in a rubbish heap by his ignorant tormentors, rescued by a native follower, and finally given to the people where it has become a classic.

[Willis R.] Hotchkiss of Africa illustrates the serious difficulties that must be overcome in giving the Word to ignorant, savage peoples. Sometimes they have no name that can be used for God, no words for virtue, home, duty. For two long years Hotchkiss lived among his Africans, eagerly seeking some word for Savior and for the idea. At last he found his word when around the camp-fire his "boys" were recounting the exciting rescue of one of their number from drowning in the river during the events of the day...

John Williams, the Master Missionary of the South Seas, tells how the Raratongans received him, when after four years of toil, he was able to return from England with the Bible in their tongue: "Everyone was eager to buy a copy. One man, as he secured his, hugged the book in ecstasy; another and another kissed it; others held them up and waved them in the air. Some sprang away like an arrow, and did not stop until they entered their own dwellings, and exhibited their treasures to their wives and children, while others jumped and danced about like persons half frantic with joy."

One of the tragedies in the Bible story has its scene in our own country. In 1831, four Nez-Perce Indians arrived in St. Louis from far-away Idaho, asking, "Where is the white man's Book of Heaven?" of which they had somehow learned. They did not know whom to seek for information and help and fell in with some of the reckless, drinking, gambling adventurers then so plentiful in border towns. After pathetic ridicule, they at length found friends and sympathy but no "Book of Heaven" that they could understand; and it was exactly forty years before the Bible was published in the dialect of the Nez-Perce. Two of the four men took sick and died in St. Louis. The other two received courtesies and promises, and with mingled grief and hope, turned homeward. Their visit did hasten the splendid missionary labors of the Methodists and Congregationalists in "the Northwest Country."

***

These sample stories suggest the fascination and the power of the Scriptures and their fitness to meet the religious need of the human heart the world over. They help us to understand how the Bible outsells every other book in Japan, China and India as well as in America, England and Canada. In 1916, the Chinese bought more than two and a quarter million copies of God's good message. The Bible is, at least in some part, now accessible to all who can read their own languages among seven-eighths of the human race. In order to reach the remaining peoples, a thousand dialects must be conquered and used to carry the "beautiful words, wonderful words of life" which "Christ the Blessed One gives to all."

DAY 43
Excerpts About Missions: Part 1 of 3
by Samuel Dickey (S. D.) Gordon
(Excerpted from *Quiet Talks on Following the Christ*, published by Fleming H. Revell Company, New York, New York in 1913)

Excerpt 1

One day I watched two young men, a Japanese and an American, pacing the deck of a Japanese liner bound for San Francisco. Their heads were close together and bent down, and they were talking earnestly. The Japanese was saying, "Oh, yes, I believe all that as a theory, but is there power to make a man live it?"

He was an officer of the ship, one of the finest boats on the Pacific. The American was a young fellow who had gone out to Japan as a government teacher, and when his earnest sort of Christianity led to his dismissal, he remained, and still remains, as a volunteer missionary. With his rare gift in personal touch he had won the young officer's confidence and was explaining what Christianity stood for, when the Japanese politely interrupted him with his question about power. The tense eagerness of his manner and voice let one see the hunger of his heart. He had high ideals of life, but confessed that every time he was in port, the shore temptations proved too much, and he always came back on board with a feeling of bitter defeat. He had read about Christianity and believed it good in theory. But he knew nothing of its power.

Through his new American friend he came into personal touch with Christ, then and there. And up to the day we docked he put in his spare time bringing other Japanese to his friend's stateroom, and there more than one of them knelt and came into warm touch of heart with the Lord Jesus. Just so our Lord Jesus draws people, Oriental and Occidental alike. Just in this way He drew people when

He was down here. He had great drawing power. People came eagerly wherever they could find Him.

Excerpt 2

A Scottish lady missionary in India tells of a Bible class of girls which she had. She was teaching them about the life and character of the Lord Jesus. One day a new girl came in, fresh from the heathenism in which she grew up, knowing nothing of the gospel. She listened and then became quite intense and excited in her childish way as she heard them talking about some One, how good He was, how gentle, how He was always teaching and helping the people around Him. At last she could restrain her eagerness no longer, but blurted out, "I know that man; he lives near us." It was found that she did not know about Christ, but supposed they were speaking of a very earnest native Christian man living in her neighborhood. She had mistaken her neighbor for Jesus. How glad that man must have been if he ever knew. This was a part of our Lord's plan.

And at the very end, these successive invitations took the shape of a command, which was both a permission and an order, "Go." People who had taken to heart, one after another, these invitations were ready for the command. They would be eager for it. The invitations were the Master's preparation for the command. He could trust such people to go, and to keep steady and true as they went, in the power He gave them.

There is one word that you find in all these invitations: "Me." They all center about the Lord Jesus. He is the center of gravity drawing everyone, in ever-growing nearness and meaning to Himself. It is only when we have been drawn into closest touch with Him that we are qualified to "go" to others. It's only Himself in us, only as much of Himself as is in us, that will be helpful to anyone else or will make anyone else willing to break with their old ways. He is the only magnet to draw people away from the old life up to Himself.

DAY 44
Excerpts About Missions: Part 2 of 3
by Samuel Dickey (S.D.) Gordon
(Excerpted from *Quiet Talks on Following the Christ*, published by Fleming H. Revell Company, New York, New York in 1913)

Excerpt 3

The story is told of a missionary in some part of Africa who had little success in his work. He was in the habit of explaining some portion of the New Testament to the people at his house. One day the portion contained the words, "give to him that asks you, and from him that would borrow from you turn not away." The people asked him if this meant what it said. He told them that it did. One of them said he would like to have the table, pointing to it; another asked for a chair, another for the bed, and so on. The missionary was rather startled at such literal taking of his teaching. He told them to come again tomorrow, and he would give his answer. When they had gone, he and his wife had a rather heart-searching time together. They felt they had not reached the hearts of the people yet. But to do as they asked meant real sacrifice of a very personal sort. At last with much prayer they decided to meet the people where they had opened the way. And so the next day they gave their answer, and soon the house was literally bare of all its furnishings. And that night they slept on the floor, yet with a sweet peace in their hearts in the midst of this strange experience.

The next day the people came back, carrying the furniture. They had really been testing these newcomers. "Now," they said, "we believe you. You live your Book. We want you to teach us." And with open hearts they listened anew to the gospel story, and many of them accepted Christ. The little incident reveals the unity of the race. Those Africans said what England and America and all the world is saying, "Live it." Is your religion livable? What the world needs today is a Jesus that lived, not simply taught, nor preached about, but lived in the power of the Holy Spirit. How the fire, the holy fire of that sort of thing would catch and spread! Oh, yes, it might mean sleeping on the bare floor! That's what living it means, the actual life overriding any mere thing that stands in the way.

Excerpt 4

I stood one day on the abrupt edge of a little hill in a Southern Japanese city. There, in a great tree hanging out over the edge, had hung the bell that called together the faithful attendants of the lord of the province when they were needed. There, nearly thirty years ago, a little band of Japanese youth of noble families, had gone out at break of day one Sabbath morning and solemnly promised to follow the Lord Jesus and to devote their lives to making Him known throughout their land. Most of them were boys still in their tender teens. And that promise was not lightly made, for already the fires of persecution had been kindled, and these fires burned fiercely but could not compete with the fire in their hearts. And as one goes up and down the island empire of the Pacific today, traces of their lives are found cropping up everywhere, like gold veins above the soil.

And as I sought to trace the hidden springs of the power at work behind all this, I found it was in the life of one young man, a simple, holy life burning with a passion for Jesus. In this life could be found the kindling of the tender flames burning so hotly in these young hearts. He was a young American officer engaged by the feudal lord of the province to teach military tactics and English. He dared not teach Christianity; that would have meant instant dismissal. So for two years he lived the message, so simply and lovingly that he won the love of his pupils. Then they came Sundays to his house to hear him read the English Bible, because they loved him. As he prayed the tears would run down his face, and they laughed to think a man would weep, but they came because they loved him. He really loved them into the Christian life.

Excerpts About Missions: Part 3 of 3
by Samuel Dickey (S. D.) Gordon
(Excerpted from *Quiet Talks on Following the Christ*, published by Fleming H. Revell
Company, New York, New York in 1913)

Excerpt 5

I recently saw a news item telling how many million copies of the Bible are being printed every year. The item insultingly remarked that the statisticians didn't seem concerned yet with figuring up how many of them were read. But, I thought, what these Bibles need is a new binding. The Bible I carry is bound in the best seal-skin with kid lining. It is supposed to be the best binding for hard wear.

But there's a much better sort of leather than that for Bible binding; I mean *shoe leather*. The people want the Bible bound in shoe leather. When we tread this Bible out in our daily walk, when what we are becomes an illustrated copy of the Bible, the greatest revival the earth has known will come. With utmost reverence let me say that our Lord Jesus wants to come and walk around in our shoes and live inside our garments and touch people through us.

Excerpt 6

A missionary returning to his homeland on furlough noted on his first return home that what had been considered luxuries before he left, were now reckoned necessities; on his second furlough he noted again that what had been reckoned luxury on his first return was now counted necessity. And each return home found this condition repeating itself.

It reminded me of the experience of Sir John Franklin in one of his Arctic explorations. His ship was trapped by an ice-field so that progress was impossible. All he could do was to calculate his longitude and latitude, and wait. The next day he was still trapped, and so far as he could see, was exactly where he had been on the previous day. But on calculating longitude and latitude again, he was surprised to find that the ship had drifted several miles backward from the position of the previous day.

It would be a sensible thing for us to make frequent calculations and find out where we are, and prayerfully steer a changed course if we've been drifting. But we can't decide such questions for each other, and they can't be decided by what another does. They can only be decided alone on one's knees with the Master, with the Book, and perhaps a map of the world at hand. We need both the Word of God and a view of the world of God to shape our judgment. No, it's not a question of money primarily, nor of missions, only of personal loyalty to our Lord Jesus, and to the passion of His heart.

DAY 46
Latin America: The Protestants
by Hubert W. Brown
(Excerpted from *Latin America: The Pagans, The Papists, The Patriots, The Protestants and the Present Problem*, published by Fleming H. Revell Company, New York, New York in 1901)

John C. Brigham, having left the United States on July 25, 1823, took three months to arrive in Buenos Aires. Once there he traveled across South America and visited the principal cities of Chile, Peru and Ecuador, and then entered Mexico by Acapulco. After two months in the Mexican capital he returned to New York. In his report of the two years' trip, while commenting on the need for gospel work, he states that the humanitarian results of liberation from Spain were most noticeable in Buenos Aires, which had been practically free for fifteen years or more. Chile had not advanced so far, and Peru very little. While many [Roman Catholic] priests favored independence, the higher clergy were attached to Spain. The work of emancipation from Catholic payments had begun. Even in Peru, much of the money formerly lavished on the church was used to support hospitals and schools. One of the latter was opened in the old Inquisition building. In Mexico our traveler noticed the "imposing worship, corrupt priesthood and superstitious people." Mr. Brigham finally decided that, "although there are many individuals in South America who have noble and expanded views on all subjects, men who are up with the spirit of the age, still there is in that field a putrid mass of superstition on which the sun of liberty must shine still longer before we can safely enter in and labor. We must wait patiently a little longer until the Ruler of nations, who has worked such wonders in these countries during the last ten years (1825) shall open still wider the way and bid us go forward."

Mr. James Thomson was an agent both of the British and Foreign Bible Society, and of a British and Foreign School Society. As the agent of the Lancasterian [advanced students teaching younger students] schools he met with a favorable reception from the civil authorities, and thus saw the prospect in a somewhat brighter light. His letters, afterwards published, were written from South America in the years 1820 to 1825. In his efforts to establish schools, Mr. Thomson secured the cooperation of many prelates [bishop or higher] of the Roman Catholic Church. Some of these went so far as to speak favorably of his circulation of the Bible in Spanish and its translation into Indian languages...In 1820 Mr. Thomson gathered 100 boys in a Lancasterian school in Buenos Aires, and taught them to read, using Scripture passages as the text. Several hundred copies of the New Testament were also circulated. One was obtained by a Patagonian chief who said he would explain it to his tribe. Schools were also established in Chile...In Lima a convent was turned over to be used as a school. "The order for the friars to vacate was given on Saturday; on Monday they began to move, and on Tuesday the keys were delivered up." The Bible also was publicly sold at "a short distance from the place where the dreadful Inquisition used to sit."...

Not only in Lima did parents ask for copies of the Word, and priests encourage its study. From Ecuador, a friend, engaged in the work of distribution, wrote to Mr. Thomson: "With pleasure have I seen in passing through the streets of Guayaquil, not once or twice, but mostly every day, the shopkeepers and the poor people who have stalls, were reading the blessed gospel of our Lord and Savior Jesus Christ. If I had had ten times as many [New Testaments] I am persuaded I could have sold them all." Thousands of copies of the New Testament were sold in Spanish, often with the help of Roman Catholic priests, and a translation of the New Testament was made into Quichua, a native language spoken by more than a million Indians. No wonder the enthusiastic Bible agent felt that "great and happy changes" were being accomplished of a kind impossible under Spanish rule, and that, "what is going forward in these countries is truly a revolution in every sense of the word."

DAY 47
A Missionary Ministry: Part 1 of 4
by Andrew Murray

(Excerpted from *The Key to the Missionary Problem*. In response to the content of the Ecumenical Missionary Conference in New York in April 1900. Published by Morrison and Gibb, Edinburgh, Scotland in 1902)

"To the pastor belongs the privilege and responsibility of the foreign missionary problem." These words point, in connection with the ministry, to a high honor, a serious shortcoming, an urgent duty, and the great need of seeking from God the grace needed to fulfill its purpose. We need not seek to allocate exactly the measure of responsibility between the ministry and the membership of the Church; all are agreed that on the ministry a holy and heavy responsibility rests in this matter. Let all ministers heartily admit and accept it and prepare themselves to live up to it.

Let us try, first of all, to find the ground on which that responsibility rests. The principles out of which it grows are simple and yet of inconceivable importance. They are these four:

1. That missions are the chief end of the Church;
2. That the chief end of the ministry is to guide the Church in this work, and equip her for it;
3. That the chief end of the preaching in a congregation ought to be to train it to take its part in helping the Church to fulfill her destiny; and
4. That the chief end of every minister in this connection ought to be to seek grace to equip themselves thoroughly for this work.

Let no one think these statements are exaggerated. They appear so because we have been so accustomed to give missions a very minor place in our thoughts of the Church and its ministry. We always need to be brought back to the great central truth, "the mystery of God," that the Church is the body of Christ, as absolutely and exclusively ordained by God to carry out the purpose of His redeeming love in the world as Christ the Head Himself. The Church has, even as Christ, just one objective for being—to be the light of the world. As Christ died for every person, as God wills that all people should be saved, so the Spirit of God in the Church knows no objective but this—that the gospel be brought to every creature. Missions are the chief end of the Church. All the work of the Holy Spirit in converting sinners and sanctifying believers has this for its one aim—to equip them for the part that each must at once take in winning back the world to God. Nothing less than what God's eternal purpose and Christ's dying love aimed at can be the aim of the Church.

As we see this to be true, we shall see that the chief end of the ministry ought to be to prepare the Church for this. Paul writes:

> God gave pastors and teachers for the perfecting of the saints unto (as to what these saints have to do) the work of ministering, or serving, unto (as the final aim of this work of the saints) the building up of the body of Christ [Ephesians 4:11-12].

It is through ministering, the loving service of the saints, that the body of Christ is to be gathered and built up. And the pastors and teachers are given the job to perfect [mature] the saints for this work of ministering…Each congregation is meant to be a training class. Every believer, without exception, is to be "perfected," to be thoroughly prepared for the work of ministering and taking part in labor and prayer for those near and far off. In all the pastor's teaching of repentance and conversion, of obedience and holiness, this definitely ought to be the supreme aim—to call people to come and serve God in the noble, holy, Christ-like work of saving the lost and restoring God's kingdom on earth. The chief end of the Church is of necessity the chief end of the ministry.

DAY 48
A Missionary Ministry: Part 2 of 4
by Andrew Murray
(Excerpted from *The Key to the Missionary Problem*. In response to the content of the Ecumenical Missionary Conference in New York in April 1900. Published by Morrison and Gibb, Edinburgh, Scotland in 1902)

The chief end of preaching ought to be to train every individual believer and every congregation to take its part in helping the Church to fulfill her destiny. This will decide the question as to how often a missionary sermon ought to be preached. As long as we only speak of one every year, it is likely that the chief thought will be obtaining a better collection of funds. This may often be obtained without the spiritual life being raised one bit. When missions take their true place as the chief aim of the Church, of which the missionary spirit has really taken possession, there may be times when a minister will feel it needed, time after time, to return to the one subject, until the neglected truth begins to master at least some in the congregation. At times, again, it may be that while there is no direct preaching on missions, yet all the teaching on love and faith, on obedience and service, on holiness and conformity to Christ, may be inspired by this one truth—that we are to be "imitators of God, and walk in love, even as Christ loved and gave Himself as a sacrifice for us." Missions are the chief end of the Church, and therefore of the ministry, and therefore all of its preaching.

All this now leads up to what, in view of the responsibility of the minister, is the main point that must be stressed, that the chief aim of every minister ought to be to prepare one's self for this great work...To inspire and train and help believers is not an easy thing; it does not come from the mere fact of being an earnest Christian, and having had ministerial training. It is a matter to which a larger emphasis ought to be given in our theological seminaries. But even this can only be partial and preparatory. The minister who would successfully combat the selfishness that is content with personal salvation, the worldliness that has no idea of sacrificing all or even anything for Christ, the unbelief that measures its power to help or bless by what it feels and sees, and not by what God and His Spirit can work, and so would lift the Church to know and rejoice in and fulfill her heavenly calling, will find the need of special training to be equipped for this the highest and holiest part of the vocation.

If the question is asked how the minister is thus to be equipped for carrying out this responsibility, the first answer will usually be, and we may take it first, "By study."

***

"Must the pastor approach the systematic study of missions?" It can only be because one knows how often, in the study of the Bible or theology, everything is simply regarded as a matter of the intellect, leaving the heart unblessed. It is possible for a person to study and know the Theory and History of Missions, and yet lack the inspiration that knowledge was meant to give. Let no pastor say that they surely know how to study. To study nature with wonder and reverence and humility is a great gift—how much more is all this needed in the higher region of the spiritual world, and especially in this, the highest spiritual truth in regard to the destiny of the Church, "the mystery of God"!

***

DAY 49
A Missionary Ministry: Part 3 of 4
by Andrew Murray

(Excerpted from *The Key to the Missionary Problem*. In response to the content of the Ecumenical Missionary Conference in New York in April 1900. Published by Morrison and Gibb, Edinburgh, Scotland in 1902)

What is it a pastor will need to study? In the missionary problem there are three great factors: the world in its sin and misery; Christ in His dying love; and the Church as the link between the two.

The first thing is to study the world. Take some of the statistics that tell of its population. Think, for instance, of some three million of the heathen dying every month—dropping over the precipice in the gloom of thick darkness at the rate of more than one every second. Or take some book that brings you face to face with the sin and degradation and suffering of some special country. Take, for instance, a book like *Across India at the Dawn of the Twentieth Century*, by Miss Lucy Guinness. I know of no book that, by its diagrams, its maps with letter-press [primary type of printing until the 20th century], its statistics, so compels the readers to stop and ask whether they believe, whether they feel what they have read. Pause and meditate and pray, asking God to give you an eye to see and a heart to feel that misery.

Think of these 300 million, that they are your British fellow-subjects. Look at the picture of that person worshipping, with a reverence many a Christian knows little of, a cobra cut in stone, until you take in what it means and cannot forget it. That person is your brother or sister. They have, like you, natures formed for worship. They do not, like you, know the true God. Will you not sacrifice everything, sacrifice yourself, to save them? Study, sometimes in its great whole, sometimes in its detail, the state of the world, until you begin to feel that God has placed you in this dark world with the one object of studying that darkness, and living and helping those who are dying in it.

And if at times you feel that it is more than you can bear, cry to God to help you to look again, and yet again, until you know that the need of the world makes it the very place where you choose to dwell. But remember always that the strongest intellect, the most vivid imagination, the most earnest study, cannot give you the right sense of these things—nothing but the Spirit and love of Jesus, waited for to make you feel what He feels, and love as He loves.

Then comes the second great lesson: Christ's love, dying for these sinners, and now longing to have won them for Him. Oh, do not think you know that dying love, that love resting on and thirsting for every creature on earth! If it takes time, and a humble, reverent, loving spirit to enter into the meaning and spirit of nature and its beauty, what do you think, my fellow minister, is it an easy thing to enter into the Holiest of All, the sanctuary of God's love, and indeed have it possess our hearts? Love is needed in the poet who would pursue the secrets of nature. The divine love, Christ's love for every creature, can only be known and felt by the loving heart that gives itself up to it, that reverently waits for it as it pleases to make itself known. If you would study the missionary problem, study it in the heart of Jesus. The missionary problem is a personal one that is meant for every believer. But it is especially true of the minister, who is to be the pattern, the teacher of believers. Study, experience, confirm the power of the personal relationship, that you may be able to teach this well—the deepest secret of true mission work.

DAY 50
A Missionary Ministry: Part 4 of 4
by Andrew Murray

(Excerpted from *The Key to the Missionary Problem*. In response to the content of the Ecumenical Missionary Conference in New York in April 1900. Published by Morrison and Gibb, Edinburgh, Scotland in 1902)

With Christ's love there is His power. Study this until the vision of a triumphant Christ, with every enemy at His feet, has cast its light upon the whole earth. The whole work of saving people is Christ's work, as much today as on Calvary, as much with each individual conversion as atonement for the sins of all. His Divine power carries on the work in and through His servants.

In studying the possible solution for the problem, in any case of special difficulty, beware of leaving out the omnipotence of Jesus. Humbly, reverently, patiently worship Him, until Christ's love and power become the inspiration of your life.

And the third great lesson to study is the Church, the connecting link between the two, between the dying Savior and the dying world. And here some of the deepest mysteries of the missionary problem will be found: That the Church should really be the Body of Christ on earth, the Head in heaven, as indispensable to Him as He is to it! That His omnipotence and His infinite redeeming love should have linked themselves for the fulfilment of His desires to the weakness of His Church! That the Church should now these hundred years have heard the preaching—missions, the supreme end of the Church! And yet be so content with a state in which that end is not counted the supreme thing! And that the Lord should yet be waiting to prove most wonderfully how truly He counts His Church as one with Himself, and ready to fill her with His Spirit and power and glory! And that there is abundant ground for a confident faith that the Lord is able and waiting to restore the Church to its pentecostal state, and so fit it for carrying out its pentecostal commission!

In the midst of such study there will grow up the clearer conviction of how the Church really is His Body, infused with the power of His Spirit, the true partaker of His Divine love, the blessed partner of His life and His glory. Faith will be awakened when the Church and its members see the evil and believe in the Divine possibility of deliverance, and then arise and give themselves in true renunciation of all to their Lord, then pentecostal glory can still return.

The world in its sin and woe, Christ in His love and power, the Church as the link between the two—these are the three great magnitudes the minister must know if he is to master the missionary problem. In study you may have to go to Scripture, and to missionary literature, and to books on theology or the spiritual life; but in the long run you will ever have to come back to the truth: the problem is a personal one. It demands a most complete and unreserved giving up of the whole being to live for that world, for that Christ, for that Church. And it demands, as we have already shown, that that personal surrender shall not merely be that of a student who is determined to master some human problem, but of one who, like a true observer of nature, gives himself or herself humbly, reverently, lovingly, to wait, and gaze, and listen until the spirit-world unlocks its secrets.

The living Christ can manifest Himself; He can, to the repentant, patient supplicant, impart His love in its power. He can make His love ours, that we may feel as He does. He can let the light of His love fall on the world, to reveal at once its need and its hope. He can give the experience in the soul of how close and how real is His union with the believer, and how divinely He can dwell and work in us.

The missionary problem is a personal one, to be solved by the power of Christ's love.

DAY 51
The Problem of Foreign Missions: Part 1 of 4
by Henry Drummond
(Excerpted from *The New Evangelism and Its Relation to Cardinal Doctrines,* published by Dodd, Mead and Company in New York, New York in 1899)

***

The missionary theology—it is useless disguising it—is supposed to be a very special truth, and a kind of theological modesty forbids some of our strongest from considering it conceivable that they should ever aspire to be missionaries. Now this feeling is very real, but I am convinced that it is very ignorant—ignorant of the changed standpoint from which scores of our missionaries are even now doing their work, ignorant of the world's real needs, ignorant of the hospitality which they would receive from many of the officials of most of the mission boards. And yet these boards are not wholly guiltless of having made it appear, or permitting it to continue to be understood, that only those of a certain type need look for welcome at their doors. I am not referring to any particular church; but I do not think the mission committees of the world have ever worded an advertisement for people in language modern enough to include the class of whom I speak. I am not arguing for free-lancers, or budding sceptics, or rationalists being turned loose on our mission fields.

But there ought to go out a new and more gracious call for young people—and our colleges were never richer in them than at this moment—who combine with all modern culture the consecrated spirit and the Christ-like life; for people who are too honest to go under false pretenses to a work which, though they are not yet especially enthusiastic for it, they are entirely willing to face it. At least it ought to be understood that what qualifies today for the leading churches at home ought not to disqualify one for the work of Christ abroad, but that there is for Christian individuals of the highest originality and power a career in the foreign field that is at least as great and rational as that at home...

Always, in opening a new mission field comes the splendid work of the pioneer—the old missionary pioneer of the Sunday school picture books, who stands with their Bible under the stereotyped palm-tree, exhorting the crowd of impossible natives. These we have had in most fields now, and their work must still and always continue. But next we have these same people in settled roles, founding congregations, planting schools, and carrying on the whole evangelical work of the Christian Church. But next, among these, and gathered from these, and in addition to these, we require a further class not wholly absorbed with specific duties, or spiritual progress, or to instill Western creeds, but whose outlook goes out to a nation as a whole; individuals who in many ways...will help advance missions education, morality, and healthy progress in all that makes for righteousness. This person, besides being the missionary, is the Christian politician, the apostle of a new social order, the molder and consolidator of the State. Such a one places the accent, if such an extreme expression of a distinction may be allowed, not on the progress of a church, but on the coming of the Kingdom of God. That one is not the herald, but the prophet of the Cross...

The Christianizing of a nation such as China or Japan is an intricate ethical, philosophical and social, as well as Christian, problem; the serious taking of any new country indeed is not to be done by casual sharp-shooters bringing down a target or two here and there, but by a carefully thought-out attack upon central points, or by a patient siege, planned with all of a military tactician's knowledge. We have at present, and we shall always need—because they will always do their measure of good—devoted individuals of the sharp-shooter order who aim at single souls. But in addition to these the Kingdom of God needs people who work with a wider vision—people prepared by fullness of historical, ethnological, and sociological knowledge to become the statesmen of the Kingdom of God.

DAY 52
The Problem of Foreign Missions: Part 2 of 4
by Henry Drummond
(Excerpted from *The New Evangelism and Its Relation to Cardinal Doctrines,* published by Dodd, Mead and Company in New York, New York in 1899)

Let me briefly expand the classification already given—partly to illustrate better what I mean, but especially to furnish a few materials to help those whose eyes, when they think of their future life, sometimes turn towards distant lands.

I begin with the New Hebrides—mainly because least is known about them. The New Hebrides mission represents a class of missions differing so essentially from those of the third and fourth classes—China and Japan—that anyone who was taught to regard it as a typical mission work would be completely misguided; and for some at least a mission work of this order would be almost the last thing they would throw themselves into. For what are the real facts? The New Hebrides are a group of small islands, a few about the size of Arran [island west of Scotland], a very few others two or three times as large, the whole of no geographical importance. They are peopled by beings of probably not more than 50,000, so that they are of no political importance. This does not refer to the islands, but to the people. The islands themselves are of so great political importance at the present moment that the allegiance of Australia to England would tremble in the balance if there were any suspicion that the Home Government would hand them over to France. The population may be over or under that stated here. I have taken my figures from authorities on the spot, but any approximation to the numbers of inhabitants on these partially explored islands must be a guess.

Whether we regard their quality or quantity, they can never play any appreciable part in the world's story; and the question which would immediately rise in the mind of the person who looked at the world from the standpoint of evolution would be the direct one: Is it really worthwhile sending twenty first-rate missionaries to work this vineyard which can never contribute anything of importance to mankind? If it is replied, But is it proved that they will not? the answer is a sad one. A closer study of these islands shows that instead of increasing their population, these are dying fast. On the first which I visited, Aneityum, when the missionaries first reached it, there were some thousands of inhabitants. Today there is a bare four hundred of depressed and sickly souls. The children are swept away by the white man's epidemics almost as soon as they are born, and the missionaries tell you that the total doom of this island may be a matter of some twenty years. The very church which was built for the islanders in better days has had to be cut in two, and even the portioned half is now too large; and a small chapel is to be built to hold the remnant of this once noble flock.

It is a dismal story, but it is more than likely that it will be repeated in time to a greater or less extent, not only throughout this group, but throughout the whole of the un-Christianized South Sea Islands. At New Caledonia I found the depletion of population even more appalling; and though here and there an island may escape, the ultimate prospect is almost total obliteration. This being so, what person who entered the mission field from the standpoint from which I speak, what person who wished one's work, however small, to contribute to the permanent evolution of the world, would choose the New Hebrides for one's mission field? No one would. Yet is the conclusion then to be drawn that this mission is a mistake? There is a book by an accomplished clergyman called, *Wrong Missions to Wrong Races in Wrong Places.* Is its thesis, when it answers this question in the affirmative, correct? I should be the last to say so, though its warning is a true one. For there are missions and missions; and this mission belongs to a type which ought to be more clearly defined and acknowledged.

DAY 53
The Problem of Foreign Missions: Part 3 of 4
by Henry Drummond
(Excerpted from *The New Evangelism and Its Relation to Cardinal Doctrines,* published by Dodd, Mead and Company in New York, New York in 1899)

In the evolutionary branch of missions the previous case just analyzed has simply no place at all—no place at all. It is a mistake from first to last. But it does not belong to this class, and is not to be judged by its standards—perhaps by higher ones. It belongs to the order of the Good Samaritan. It is a mission of pure compassion. Its parallel is the mission of Father Damien on Leper Island. Who shall say that there are not, and will not always be, people among us who see that kind of mission, people who have no intellectual understanding of evolution, but who possess the kind heart? Or who will say that the day will ever come when the leaders of the wider movement will begrudge such individuals to the lost places of the earth?

I cannot leave this subject without paying my passing tribute—may I say my homage?—to the missionaries of the New Hebrides themselves. From a recent biography which all of you have read, you know something of the difficulties of their work. You remember the description of the Island of Tanna, the remoteness of its position, the strangeness of its language, the fierceness of its people; you remember how daily the savages sought the missionary's life, and how after years of facing death in a hundred forms he was driven from their shores with scarcely a single convert for his investment. Last June, sailing along Tanna, I tried to land near [John Gibson] Paton's deserted field. With me was one of the missionaries who has now gained a footing on another part of that island still populated with cannibals.

As we neared the shore, a hundred painted savages poured from out of the woods, and prepared to fire upon us with their guns and poisoned arrows. But the missionary stood up in the bow of the boat and spoke two words to them in their native tongue. Instantly every gun was laid upon the beach, and they rushed into the surf to welcome us ashore. No other unarmed man on this earth could have landed there. It meant that the foundation-stone of civilization upon Tanna was already laid. Every island was once like Tanna; some are like it still. But on one after another the cannibal spirit has been already conquered, schools are planted everywhere, and neat churches and parsonages gleam through the palm trees and signal to the few ships which wander in those seas that here at least life and property are safe.

At Eromanga I went to see the spot on the beach where [John] Williams fell. Nearby were the graves of his murdered successors, Mr. [George] and Mrs. [Ellen] Gordon. Their almost immediate successor, Mr. [H. A.] Robertson, is there today, his large church and beautiful parsonage within a stone's throw of the place where these first martyrs died; his leading elder the son of the cannibal who murdered Gordon. That monster left three sons; they are all elders of the church, and life is as safe throughout that island today as in England. For the first year of their life in Eromanga, Mr. and Mrs. Robertson lived in a bullet-proof stockade. They left it only under cover of night for a few yards, and on few occasions, once to bury their first-born baby. For a year they never saw a European. Their work was to let the people look at them. Their message was to be kind. By and by acquaintance was picked up with one or two natives, the circle of influence spread, and after years of extraordinary patience and self-denial, their lives again and again hanging by a thread, they won this island for civilization and Christianity.

On another island, where the missionary two years ago used to see the smoke of the cannibal feasts from his door-step, the natives brought me their spears and bows and poisoned arrows. "We do not need them now," they said, "the missionary has taught us not to kill."

DAY 54
The Problem of Foreign Missions: Part 4 of 4
by Henry Drummond
(Excerpted from *The New Evangelism and Its Relation to Cardinal Doctrines,* published by Dodd, Mead and Company in New York, New York in 1899)

I have no words to express my admiration for these men, and, may I say, their even more heroic wives; they are perfect missionaries, their toil has paid a hundred times; and I count it one of the privileges of my life to have been one of the few eye-witnesses of their work. As to the calls of this field for more workers, I must add this. It is a proof of the sound sense of the New Hebrides missionaries that they are pretty unanimous in agreeing that, considering the needs of the rest of the world, they have already a quite fair portion of workers. The staff, of course, could be doubled or tripled tomorrow with great advantage, but the missionaries do not ask for it. With their present resources and the number of native teachers who are in training, they hope in time to cover these islands with mission stations by themselves. I confess these are the least greedy missionaries I ever heard of…

From the old standpoint the work in China seems to be splendid. Men and women from every Christian Church in the world are busy all over the land, and small congregations of native Christians are springing up everywhere along their track. The industry and devotion of the workers—Roman Catholic, Episcopalian, Congregational, Presbyterian, Wesleyan, and a host of others—are beyond all praise, and all of the missionaries who will tell you that they are encouraged, that some fruit is seen, and that the future is full of hope. There seems to be great care, moreover, in the admission to the churches of native Christians, and the belief in education and in medical missions is widely rooted. But from the ideal of a Christian evolution, there remains very much to criticize—happily less in the direction of commission than of omission. This band of missionaries…is no steady regiment set on a fixed campaign, but a disordered host of guerillas recruited from all denominations, wearing all uniforms, and waging a random fight. Some are equipped with obsolete weapons, some with modern armament; but they possess no common program or consistent method. Besides being confusing to the Chinese, this means great waste of power, great loss of cumulative effect. This, of course, is inevitable at first, and it is not the sin of the missionaries, but of Christendom; and, after the late Shanghai conference, there is more than a hope that in time even this may be remedied.

But what one would really like to see, in addition to greater concentration, would be a more serious reconsideration of the manner of approach and the form of message most suited to the Chinese mind and nature and tradition, and some further contribution to the question how far its form of Christianity is to be Western, or how far a Chinese basis is possible or permissible. These questions might be left to adjust themselves but for one most serious fact: the converts in China, in the majority of districts, are almost exclusively drawn at present from the lower classes. There are exceptions, but the educated classes as a whole, the merchants and the mandarins [bureaucrats], remain, I understand, almost wholly untouched. There is something wrong if this is the case. And leaving the present systems to do the good work it is doing among the poor, I would join with the best of the missionaries in arguing for a few "rabbis" to be sent to China, or to be picked from our fine scholars already there, who would quietly reconnoiter the whole situation, and shape the teaching of the country along well-considered lines—individuals, especially, who would lay themselves out through education, lectures, preaching, and literature to reach the intellect of the Empire. That some are aiming at this, and doing it splendidly, we are already well aware. It is the direct policy of many missionaries and even of whole societies. But it is these missionaries themselves who are crying out for more of it.

***

DAY 55
The New Apostolate of Woman: Part 1 of 4
by Arthur T. Pierson
(Excerpted from *The New Acts of the Apostles*, published by The Baker & Taylor Company, New York, New York in 1894)

A marked feature of the "New" Acts of the Apostles is the apostolate of woman. From the day when Gabriel announced to that Virgin of Bethlehem her destiny as the human mother of the Son of God, woman has taken a new rank in history. Mary of Magdala, to whom He first appeared after His resurrection, was a forerunner of the thousands of her sex who should bear the good tidings of a risen Savior. That outcast of Samaria who forgot her water pot and hurried from the well to tell even the men of the city about the Messiah forecast the myriad women who should forget themselves and all secular cares in the ministry to souls.

These were prophecies of woman's work and have been fulfilled in a startling manner in this new era. As the new age of missions moves toward the final goal, more and more does Christian womanhood come to the front. Today, more than one-third of the entire force in the foreign field is composed of godly women. At home women's organizations, the outgrowth of the last quarter century, have had an increase so rapid, an influence so wide, and an impulse so forceful, that no other agency compares with them in value and virtue. They have created and scattered cheap and attractive leaflets on missions, stimulated consecration of home life, and trained up a new generation of self-devoted missionaries; and, amid all the variations of values and crises in the money market, kept up a constant advance in the scale of gifts to the Lord. The decided advance of missionary enterprise during the past thirty years we owe to the increased activity of these women who still follow the Master and minister to Him out of their substance.

This theme demands a separate treatment, for the field it opens is too broad to be otherwise surveyed. The bare mention of the names of the holy women, single and married, who have adorned the annals of modern missions, would require much space; but to attempt even the briefest sketch of the heroines of the mission field would demand a volume. In some cases they have been wives and mothers, like those three grand women who in succession shared the work of the devoted [Adoniram] Judson in Burma, and one of whom laid the cornerstone of Siamese [Thai] missions. Others have been single women like Fidelia Fiske in Persia, Eliza Agnew in Ceylon, Mary Whately in Cairo, Matilda Rankin in Mexico, Mary Graybell in India, and Clara Cushman in China.

Mary Moffat for a half century bore with her husband the yoke of toil and sacrifice among the Bechuanas [South Africa]. Maria Gobat for forty-five years was Samuel Gobat's invaluable helper in Abyssinia [Ethiopia] and Malta, and finally in the bishopric of Jerusalem. Hannah Mullens, daughter of one noble missionary, was the wife of another and has left her lasting footprints in Indian *Zenanas* [areas of homes in India designated for women]. Judith Grant spent but four years in Oroomiah [Iran], and was only twenty-five years old when she died, but her husband found that her life was the most powerful sermon ever preached in the land of Esther.

The work of Mary Williams is scarcely less illustrious than that of the martyr of Erromanga [John Williams]. When Dorothy Jones at twenty-four years of age returned to England from the West Indies a childless widow, after a year of service among those enslaved negroes, she had passed through a shipwreck whose frightful agonies had distorted her face beyond recognition, yet she could only say, "I have never once regretted engaging in mission work."

DAY 56
The New Apostolate of Woman: Part 2 of 4
by Arthur T. Pierson
(Excerpted from *The New Acts of the Apostles*, published by The Baker & Taylor
Company, New York, New York in 1894)

Anna Hinderer spent seventeen years by the side of her beloved
David, in the Yoruba [Nigeria] country, and so captivated the
women that they almost worshipped her, and so inspired heroism in
her converts that they endured torture for Jesus' sake. Rebecca
Wakefield spent but three years in Zanzibar [in Tanzania], but her
heroic fight with hardship and privation, and all the foes of a hostile
climate and a pagan society, won for her the crown of a courage
"loftier than that of Joan of Arc." Sarah B. Capron not only took
equal part in her husband's long service in India, but after his death
trained scores of Bible women for *zenana* work [areas of Indian
homes for women only], and has now given her maturest days, in
the Bible Institute at Chicago, to the training of candidates for
mission work, both at home and abroad.

Out of all this illustrious company of women, in the field of
missions, we take, almost at random, a few names as examples of
this modern apostolate of woman.

Hannah Catharine Lacroix Mullens was born in India. The women of
that vast peninsula were therefore doubly her sisters, and nobly did
she redeem the debt of sisterhood. As a girl of twelve she was
already about her "Father's business," teaching native girls at
Bhowanipore. At nineteen she became the wife of the Rev. Joseph
Mullens of the London Missionary Society in Calcutta, and from
that time on, the very roots of her being struck deep into the work
of a missionary and absorbed all her energy. Her aid in her
husband's study of Bengali, her work in the boarding-school for
Hindu girls and in the Bible classes for native women, her sanctified

pen as a proper companion to her anointed tongue—all these are but hints of the varied and abundant service that made that life overflow with usefulness. She has sometimes been called the pioneer of *zenana* work; but, before her day, when Rev. John Fordyce was in India, the movement for penetrating the closed doors of Hindu homes had begun; yet Mrs. Mullens has an indisputable share in the glory of securing wider access to the exiled women of India, and of winning them to Christ. And when, after sixteen years as a missionary's wife, she was suddenly called up higher, at the early age of thirty-five, her last day had been spent in writing a book for the native women.

Emily Chubbuck Judson. Long before "Fanny Forester" had met her husband, her zeal for missions had been kindled over the memoir of Ann Haseltine Judson; and when, in 1845, he first met her and asked for the service of her graceful pen in preparing the memoir of the second Mrs. Judson, either of them thought that the interview would lead to marriage. The few years of her experience in Burma were crowded with self-sacrificing service; and in 1850, when Dr. Judson's fast-failing health made a sea voyage necessary, though she scarcely knew how to breathe apart from him, and was herself in an apparent decline, she heroically stayed behind. Left with three children in her charge, and one of them her first-born infant of two years, and expecting her second experience of maternity within one month, she cheerfully bade her husband farewell. Three weeks after he sailed, she gave birth to her little "Charles," and soon after laid him in his grave, little knowing that his father had made the sea his grave ten days before his infant son had departed; for there were four months of terrible suspense before she knew whether her husband was alive or dead. Yet she leaned hard on Jesus, and, with a patient heroism which is unsurpassed in the annals of missionary life, "endured as seeing Him who is invisible!"

DAY 57
The New Apostolate of Woman: Part 3 of 4
by Arthur T. Pierson

(Excerpted from *The New Acts of the Apostles*, published by The Baker & Taylor Company, New York, New York in 1894)

Mary Chauner Williams. John Williams always said that without his wife he did not know what he would have done. Besides all her loving, conjugal and maternal ministries, her lofty spirit made even the most menial offices of cook and housemaid radiant, and in addition, she was a teacher. From her the women of Raiatea [Polynesia] learned the arts of household life, while every such lesson became a channel for higher instruction. She searched out the aged, half-nude and altogether despised and neglected, placed them under proper care, and led many of them to find a new support for their old age and a new light at life's evening-time. The younger women she diligently taught until they were trained in the words of faith and good doctrine. Whether with her husband in his "circumnavigation of charity," or staying behind to care for interests that would suffer in their absence, she was the same uncomplaining servant and burden-bearer of the Lord: and, when seven of her babies were sleeping [dead] on the various isles of the Pacific, this handmaid of the Lord could still say, "Be it unto me, according to Your word!" In poverty or peril, sickness or suffering, she was alike undaunted and undiscouraged. Awakened at midnight with the awful news of her husband's tragic death at Erromanga, and while so overcome with a paralysis of grief that even friendly visits of sympathy were a torture, she admitted, among the first who entered that chamber of sorrow, Malietoa, the chief. He was himself overwhelmed by the loss which put all Polynesia under its cloud. Frantically, he appealed to her not to kill herself by indulging grief, pleading with her to live for the sake of himself and his poor people, and crying out, "If you too are taken, O what shall we then do!"

Fidelia Fiske. Born the same year that Williams sailed for the South Seas, at twenty-seven years old, this noble woman went to reproduce in the land of Esther [Persia/Iran] the system of instruction which at Holyoke, Massachusetts, made Mary Lyon's school for girls so famous. There are various types of bravery, and none more heroic than what this refined and delicate woman displayed, as for Christ's sake she dared the unutterable filth and countless army of vermin encountered in the huts of Oroomiah.

When in 1843 she arrived in Persia, about forty schools had been opened on those plains, but for the most part reached only the boys; and the girls' school, that Mrs. Grant had founded five years earlier, dragged out a half-dead existence. This humble daughter of Shelbourne, niece of the Syrian missionary, Pliny Fiske, was to become the real pioneer of woman's education in Persia.

God laid it on her heart to lift up out of the horrible pit and miry clay of unspeakable degradation, Nestorian womanhood [a specific people in Iran]; but to do it she must herself go down into the pit. She saw that to raise womanhood, she must first lift girlhood to a higher level. So she began with the daughters and courageously took measures to gather into a family school a few whom she would cleanse and clothe, feed and train. She looked for six girls with which to begin, and, while as yet she knew but one Syriac sentence, she used that to beg parents to "give their daughters." On the proposed day of opening, though fifteen day-scholars arrived, not one "boarder" was secured. Mar-Yohanan, however, came, leading two little girls of seven and ten; and to this first "gift of daughters" additions were slowly made until they numbered twenty-five—all she could then accommodate.

DAY 58
The New Apostolate of Woman: Part 4 of 4
by Arthur T. Pierson

(Excerpted from *The New Acts of the Apostles*, published by The Baker & Taylor Company, New York, New York in 1894)

Fidelia Fiske continued...Subsequently, on foundations laid in prayers and wet with tears was reared in that New Holyoke [modeled on a Massachusetts school for girls] which has been a Persian pearl of great price. For sixteen years she carried on her apostolic work, and when illness drove her home her one wish was to get back to the land of the magi. Cancer ate at her vitals until, not even fifty years old, she died, in 1864. Yet, while weary and worn, feeling this vulture gnawing at her heart, she not only pleaded ceaselessly for missions, but actually took the principal's position at Holyoke, Massachusetts, so that with her dying hand she might still sow the seeds of missionary consecration in youthful soil.

Of Fidelia Fiske the venerable secretary of the American Board has said: "In the structure and working of her whole nature she seemed to me the nearest approach I ever saw, in man or woman, to my ideal of our beloved Savior as He appeared on earth."

The work which began with the repulsive task of literally cleansing from filth and purging of vermin the very bodies of Persian girls, found its reward when, in the three years from 1844 to 1847, an outpouring so abundant fell upon her school that it could be compared to nothing but the first Pentecost. All the girls over twelve years were converted, and many of them became missionaries in these Persian homes. The school was so obviously blessed in lifting women above the low level of the donkey, and elevating that character which is the secret of all improved condition, that persecution only showed its worth and multiplied its supporters and necessitated larger rooms. During the closing days of Miss Fiske's stay in Oroomiah, ninety-three converted women, in one meeting, greeted her as first-fruits of a life whose motto was, "Live for Christ."

We may well thank God that, after being kept in the background for centuries, Christian womanhood is finding its true sphere of work and is wielding its golden scepter of influence. Missions have shown the normal status of women in the Church and in the world; and how closely their identification with their Redeemer is also linked with family life and social life, so that without them there can be no holy household or reformed society. And their deep sense of infinite debt to Christ, not only for salvation, but for them redemption from their domestic and social bondage, prompts them to undertake a mission to their abused sisters in pagan, heathen and Muslim lands, which can by no one but a Christian woman be done at all. Perhaps God suffered *zenanas* and harems to be locked against men so that women might feel more clearly His providential call for their service to their sex.

No human gauge can measure women's work for women. When Dr. Eli Smith of Syria was giving theological students his reasons why, ordinarily, missionaries should take a wife, he spoke not only of their contribution to their husbands' home comforts and their power to shelter him from moral suspicion, but he added with earnest emphasis that the wife quite often does as effective work in the foreign field as her husband, and that nothing is needed more as a living lesson to these degraded and ignorant idolaters and victims of vicious social surroundings, than the practical exhibition in the Christian woman herself of what the religion of Christ does for her as a daughter and sister, wife and mother. The common witness of the most heroic and successful missionaries is that the holy lives and tireless labors of devoted women have been indispensable to the highest results of missions. There was a time when women were regarded as little more than man's helper, if not servant: but Paul wrote, "Help those women which labored with us in the gospel" [Philippians 4:3], as though they were now leaders, and the men were to go to their help!

DAY 59
The Transformations of Grace: Part 1 of 3
by Arthur T. Pierson
(Excerpted from *The Crisis of Missions*, published by Robert Carter and Brothers,
New York, New York in 1886)

It is one of the mysterious sayings of prophecy, that in the golden age that is coming, even the wolf, bear, leopard, and lion are to be led by a little child. Already we have foretastes of the fulfilment of this prediction. That little child born in Bethlehem, who, in all His manly, godly growth in wisdom and stature and in favor with God and people, never lost the childlike spirit, takes by the hand and leads others as predatory as the wolf, as treacherous as the leopard, as ferocious as the bear or the lion.

When Robert Moffat proposed to go to [Jager] Afrikaner [criminal], the terrible demon of the Dark Continent, he was warned that he was an incarnate fiend, who would make a virtue of cruelty, and murder him so that he might make a drum-head of his skin and a drinking-cup of his skull. But Moffat had faith in the gospel of the grace of God. This Hottentot chief had been driven north by Dutch invaders until, taking his refuge beyond the Orange River, he became a daring and desperate outlaw, robbing and murdering his victims, and controlling a wide region with the iron scepter of terror. The colonial governments set a price upon his capture, dead or alive, and hired neighboring chiefs to make war upon him; but in vain. In 1818 Moffat ventured to live with Afrikaner. A change took place in the diabolical thug, so complete that it was a new creation. His outward and inward life was transformed; he became a man of peace; the helper, friend, nurse of the missionary; a student of the New Testament, an evangelist in spirit, a winner of souls. Robert Moffat's success was based on his confidence in the power of the gospel to tame the fiercest and most ferocious people, and he saw that man, who in himself combined wolf, bear, leopard, and lion, turned into a lamb.

What hope could there be for a South Sea islander who, in pure malice of cruelty, first slew his little brother without pity, and then sent the corpse to his king for a sacrifice! Dead to love, alive only to hate, making sport of murder, and murder a sport! Yet he is but a representative—as Paul would say, "a pattern"—of thousands out of whom, as from him, have been cast out a legion of demons.

Sau Quala, the Karen [ethnic group in Burma] slave, was by that same gospel brought to Christ as the first Karen convert, and then changed into an apostolic worker. He aided the missionaries in the translation of the Word, and for fifteen years guided them through the jungles in their missionary journeys in Tavoy and Mergui; then his holy zeal could no longer be pent up, and he began to walk through the country preaching, gathering converts, planting churches, within three years organizing nearly twenty-five hundred new disciples into over thirty congregations. His work was one of love, performed in the most heroically unselfish spirit; his voluntary poverty compelled him to leave his lovely wife behind him, because he could not afford the luxury of her companionship; and, in the face of the offer of a lucrative government position, he continued his self-denying labor, refusing to mix up secular labor with the Lord's work. Dr. Anderson closes his little biographical sketch of this Karen apostle with the exclamation, "Admirable man! Where shall we find his equal in devotion to the cause of Christ!" Yet from what depths of ignorance, selfishness, and superstition, the gospel lever lifted Sau Quala!

DAY 60
The Transformations of Grace: Part 2 of 3
by Arthur T. Pierson
(Excerpted from *The Crisis of Missions*, published by Robert Carter and Brothers,
New York, New York in 1886)

During the revival in Fidelia Fiske's Holyoke school in Persia, Guergis, "the vilest of the Nestorians," came to visit his daughter in the school. He was in full Kurdish dress, with gun and dagger. As the girls wept and prayed, he sneered and mocked. His daughter prayed for him. He raised his fist to strike her, but the Lord held it back. Miss Fiske sought to win him, but he continued to laugh and scorn for days. Then suddenly, as if by a lightning-stroke, he was struck down. He wept and prayed, went away to be alone with God, and came back an entirely changed man. The gun and dagger were no more to be seen. Bowed down with the weight of his sin, he declared that even "if there were no hell he could not bear such a load." He found rest in believing, and from then on all he could say was, "My great sins and my great Savior!" Even Miss Fiske, stunned by the miracle of such a conversion, doubted his sincerity. But until his death, Deacon Guergis continued with lips and life to tell of Jesus. You might have met him travelling along the mountains, in his red trousers, striped jacket, and big turban, with Testament and hymn-book in place of gun and dagger, talking of sin and salvation, and singing with booming voice, "Rock of Ages," "There is a Fountain," etc. On his dying bed he would rouse up and shout, "Oh, it was free grace, free grace!"

U. Bor. Sing, the heir of the Rajah of Cherra, India, was converted by Welsh missionaries. He was warned that in joining the Christians he would probably forfeit his right to be King of Cherra after the death of Rham Sing, who then ruled, but who, eighteen months afterward, died. The chiefs of the tribes met and unanimously decided that Bor. Sing was entitled to succeed him, but that his

Christian profession stood in the way. Messenger after messenger was sent, urging him to recant. He was invited to the native council, and told that if he would put aside his religious profession they would all acknowledge him as king. His answer was: "Put aside my Christian profession? I can put aside my head-dress, or my cloak; but as for the covenant I have made with my God, I cannot for any consideration put that aside!" Another was therefore appointed king in his stead. Since then he has been impoverished by litigation about property, until he is now in danger of arrest and imprisonment; and Mr. Elliott, the Commissioner of Assam, has appealed to Christians in this country on his behalf. Here is a convert rejecting a crown for Christ!

Rev. John Thomas, of the Church Missionary Society, has said of a convert among the Shanars [later known as Nadars, a low caste of India] who died in 1860, that he was, without exception, the ablest and most eloquent native preacher in India. "His affection, simplicity, honesty, straightforwardness, amazing pulpit talents, and profound humility, endeared him to me more than I can describe," said this beloved missionary, who also declared that his last sermon on the text, "enduring the cross, despising the shame," the greatest sermon he ever heard in its exaltation of Christ and its overwhelming effect.

"Blind Bartimeus" of the Hawaiian islands, is another example of transforming grace. Out of the lowest depths of pagan vice and vileness he rose to a level with the most earnest, consecrated, self-oblivious [unmindful of self] disciples and laborers. His wonderful insight into the truth, his inspired imagination, his white-heat of devotion and intensity, his contagious enthusiasm, his passionate love for souls, enabled him to preach the most severe truths with the tenderness of an angel; and his familiarity with the Word of God made him, blind as he was, a walking concordance.

DAY 61
The Transformations of Grace: Part 3 of 3
by Arthur T. Pierson

(Excerpted from *The Crisis of Missions*, published by Robert Carter and Brothers, New York, New York in 1886)

There is not a missionary field where such triumphs of grace may not be constantly seen; transformations of character quite as marvelous and as absolutely unexplainable without a divine factor, as any miracle of apostolic days. Dr. Lindley used to say that when a native Zulu, trading some trifling article for a calico shirt, duck breeches [type of pants], and a three-legged stool, got his shirt and breeches on and sat on his little stool, he was a thousand miles above all his fellows. But this is only civilization. We must follow that poor Zulu, just clothed, until the Word of God takes root in their souls, and they become not only beautiful and fruitful in holiness, but preachers and winners of souls, giving the life that has been plucked as a burning stick from the fire of an earthly hell, to be consumed on the altar of Christian service; and then we begin to understand how much farther the transforming influences of Christianity reach than those of mere civilization.

The Portuguese called the Hottentots [non-Bantu tribe of South Africa] "a race of apes," and Dr. Vanderkemp read over church-doors in Cape Colony, "Dogs and Hottentots not admitted." Yet out of those Hottentots what disciples have been developed!

***

The first messenger of Christ to carry the Bible into Korea and offer it to the king was a Chinese convert. The noblest examples of self-denial, separation unto God, passion for souls, singleness of aim, evangelistic zeal, and liberal systematic giving which have been found during this century, have been the outgrowth of missionary fields, and often of the most hopeless soil, previously rank with every unholy product. The new converts from the most degraded tribes have often put to shame the ripest fruits of our Christian civilization!

In January, 1872, during the week of prayer, one or two Japanese converts, recently brought to Christ and taught in the private classes of the missionaries, came into the English meeting at Yokohama. There they heard read and explained the story of that first Pentecost from the book of the Acts of the Apostles. They fell on their knees as though themselves were set on fire with pentecostal flames, and with prayers like those of Daniel and Paul, begged God to pour out the Spirit in a new Pentecost upon Japan until even the captains of the English and American warships wept and said, "The prayers of these new Japanese converts take the heart out of us"...

Conversion in China is followed by exactly the same fruits as in all the rest of the world. They demonstrate in love to all the saints in word and in deed. Next to the love of Christ, which reigns supreme, this sympathy and large-hearted active charity to persecuted brethren in other places is noteworthy. Before conversion they cared nothing about suffering people elsewhere; but now, hearing that some whom they have never seen are driven from their homes for Christ's sake, they are ready to share with them what little they have. "The crucial test of a man's faith in China is his rejection of ancestral worship for himself after death. An old Christian called his idol-worshipping sons to his bedside, and, gathering all his remaining strength in one last effort, instructed them to send for the Christians to read the Scriptures at his funeral, and pray and sing about the resurrection, and, under pain of his displeasure, have no heathen ceremonies over him and no offerings made to him after he was gone"...Let these few individual examples, drawn from the sable sons of Africa, the Karen slaves of Burma, the wild Kurds of Persia, the superstitious Brahmins of India, the vile pagans of Polynesia, the iron-bound Confucianists of China, and the benighted Buddhists of Japan, stand as illustrations of the fact that wherever the gospel goes, its path is one of conquest. God is with His own Word, and it does not return to Him void.

DAY 62
Mission to Armenians in Turkey: Part 1 of 2
by Maria A. West

(Excerpted from *The Romance of Missions: Inside Views of Life and Labor in the Land of Ararat*, published by Anson D. F. Randolph & Company, New York, New York in 1875)

Providential Care

Haji Hagop was an early convert, and a pioneer in the work of evangelizing his countrymen. His dignified bearing and unquestioned piety, combined with a sound judgment and evenly-balanced mind, rendered him invaluable as a helper; he was known as a "peacemaker" and his counsel was widely sought by the Protestants and others. But when the infirmities of age prevented active service, and funds were low, the missionaries were obliged to cut off his small monthly allowance. "Haji Baba," or Father, as he was called, took this very meekly and gave himself the more earnestly "unto prayer." A few months later, a letter was received from an unknown friend in Holland, who had accidently seen a brief account of the circumstance in an English periodical, and was moved to send to the missionaries the sum necessary for the support of the good man.

This he continued to send every quarter until the very time when it was no longer needed; and then it suddenly ceased. Letters of inquiry failed to receive a response, as before (in the quaint and charming utterances of a child-like Christian heart and mind), forcing upon us the conviction that the benefactor also had ended his earthly mission and "entered into rest."

This remarkable provision of Providence brings to mind the experience of a missionary widow of the American Board, who, with her children, had returned to her native land. Eight or ten years had passed, and one day, at the very time when she was praying for funds to carry one of her sons through a medical course, and another through college, the "old king" of Siam was walking and talking with a missionary interpreter when, without any previous reference to the subject, he suddenly stopped and said, "By the way, where is Mrs. Caswell? I wish to send her some money!" Mr. Caswell was the king's first teacher in English, and he had seemed fond of him, but for years had not mentioned his name. The missionary, who had come at a later time, informed the king how he might safely transmit the money; and he sent Mrs. Caswell a draft for $1,500, causing the "widow's heart to sing for joy." This was subsequently followed by $500, in addition, with the photographs of the royal family. Truly, "the king's heart is in the hand of the Lord" [Proverbs 21:1].

The "Cost" of Missions
The Holy Spirit has been working among us for months past, as silently as the "dew that descended upon the mountains of Zion," and we believe that a number of these Armenian women and girls for whom we have prayed and labored are truly "born again." What joy is like our joy over souls saved for all eternity, and new workers gained for the Master's vineyard? We want no miserable, earthly calculation which estimates the "cost of conversion at $1,000" per soul! In God's arithmetic, and the wonderful economy of grace (past the comprehension of such sordid minds), each grain that we reap in these harvest fields is counted as a living seed that will bring forth fruit a hundred and a thousand fold!

Moral Courage
Experience and observation confirm the conviction that *moral courage* is one of the rarest of virtues among Christians in the present day. Many servants of Christ (like Elijah) boldly hack to pieces the priests of Baal before the Lord and then *flee from the wrath of an offended woman!*

DAY 63
Mission to Armenians in Turkey: Part 2 of 2
by Maria A. West

(Excerpted from *The Romance of Missions: Inside Views of Life and Labor in the Land of Ararat*, published by Anson D. F. Randolph & Company, New York, New York in 1875)

The Mothers Meeting

At the appointed time, forty women gathered in the chapel and sat at my feet while I read to them the story of the woman of Samaria, and in simple language, as to children, tried to unfold the "Glad Tidings" of a Savior for a poor, sinful woman. The "old, old story" was new to many of them, and it was touching to see their interest. As one and another bent forward in her eagerness to catch every word, the big tears gathered and rolled down many a wrinkled face, and dropped unheeded on the floor. And I realized more fully than ever before the blessedness of the missionary work: the high honor and sacred privilege of following in the footsteps of Him who "came, not to be ministered to, but to minister."

Suddenly, one of the women burst out with the question, "Varzhoohi, have you a mother?" "O, yes! A blessed mother," I answered. "Can she read?" asked another. "Yes, indeed; she learned to read when only four years old, and she also writes; sending many precious letters to her far-away daughter." "But how could she give you up to go so far away?" was the next question. "Because she loves you so much. She prays for you every day," I said. "Now listen, and I will tell you all about it." New interest lighted up some previously indifferent countenances as I told them of my saintly mother, how she loved Jesus, and trained her children for Him, and found in her Bible and prayer blessed comfort and support in her widowhood and the loss of three of her sons; that when the call came for me to leave all and go to a strange country in obedience to the great command, "Go into all the world, and preach the gospel to every creature," she said, though with many tears, "My child, I gave you to God in infancy, and if He calls I cannot hold you back. If one soul is saved through your work, it will repay me for the sacrifice I make in giving you up." This brief history of a mother, a woman like, and yet so unlike, themselves touched a chord which vibrated in the hearts of these simple children of nature; one and another nodded to her neighbor, wonderingly, as if to say, "What love is this? If she so cares for us, how should we care for ourselves." Then it was easy and delightful to turn their attention to that greater Love which spared not "His only begotten and well-beloved Son." Iskoohi offered a fervent prayer and the meeting was closed. But the women lingered and gathered around me for a few more words. As they were slowly leaving, one of the more aged turned back, and throwing her arms around me, exclaimed, "You are an angel sent from God to teach us!" And again I thanked God for the privilege of bringing the bread of life to those starving souls. Ah! Love was the golden key which had opened those hearts; the most potent force in the universe.

Missing Home

How we sometimes long, with unutterable yearnings, to take the wings of the morning, and spend one day, or one hour even, with friends by the old fireside! To sit down at the home table with those so far away! To gather with them around the family altar once more, or go up to the house of God in company. How good it would be to hear again a sermon from the lips of our dear old pastor! To drop in at one of the weekly church prayer meetings, and unite in the song of praise, and the fervent prayers in our sweet mother-tongue! What a rest of soul it would be to spend an evening with aged, experienced Christians who are praying, "Your kingdom come," and sit at their feet and seek counsel, and learn wisdom at their lips! Perhaps those of us who have no home, no real abiding place in this land, who, however much we may love and be loved by missionary brothers and sisters, must always in reality be "boarders," feel more intensely the isolation than others who did not leave all, in devoting themselves to this work of gospel ministry in a strange land and a strange tongue.

DAY 64
Fishers of Men: Part 1 of 3
by David James Burrell
(Excerpted from *The Golden Passion*, published by Wilbur B. Ketcham, New York, New York in 1897)

"Do not be afraid; from now on you will be catching men."
Luke 5:10

Here is Peter, a great soul if there ever was one, endowed with magnificent gifts and possibilities of usefulness. He is part owner of a little boat; he cruises up and down Gennesaret [Sea of Galilee] for fish, carries them to the marketplace at Capernaum, and bargains there with housewives for a small income. It is an honorable calling...All honest toil is honorable. But is the making of a livelihood—adequate or wealth—the consummation of life's purpose? Is this the best that Peter shall hope for? Early to bed, and early to rise, and down to the boats, and battling with the winds and waves, day in and day out, until the years are gone, and the limbs tremble, and the eyes are dim, and the hands are folded—O Peter, with your mighty soul! Is this all? And is life worth living if this is all?

Here is John; his great eyes are full of dreams and visions and apocalypses; power is hiding there. He busies himself with dragging the nets, mending their meshes, hanging them in the sun. Is there no larger place for John in the busy world than the little fishing boat? Shall all his energies be exhausted in the rigging of sails and the dragging of nets? Alas for a person whose soul is imprisoned in secular life! Alas for the lawyer who never gets above his briefs, the physician who knows no more than "laudamy and calamy" [treatments], the carpenter who is satisfied with the shoving of his saw and plane, the housewife whose soul is absorbed in her duties! We are made in God's likeness. Shall the eagle be tethered to a stake? Shall a lion be harnessed to a cart? An honest lark pie is worth a shilling, but a lark's song—as it rises from the meadow with the dew of the morning on its wings and pierces the ether and gazes toward the sun—O, a lark's song cannot be valued with the gold of Ophir. *Sursum corda* [lift up your hearts]! Up with your heart, O son of the living God! Make your secular business as honorable as you please; yet your life will be a failure if it exhausts itself upon that.

But the Master comes this way. "Follow me," is His word, "and I will make you fishers of men"; that is, "I will not turn you aside from the familiar methods of your occupation; fishers once, fishers ever. But you shall be promoted to a higher sphere; as apostles, missionaries, evangelists, teachers, you shall turn your skill to the betterment of the world." We also are in the apostolic succession. The apostles are "sent ones"; so are we. For did not the Master say, "As the Father sent Me into the world, so have I sent you"? For what? To deliver the world from its shame and sin. Blessed calling! The Master speaks. Bring all your energies of body and soul to the promotion of truth and righteousness. Seek first of all the kingdom of God.

Here also is an unveiling of the secret of power. The words of Peter are significant: "Master, we have toiled all the night; nevertheless, at Your word I will let down the net." The key of the whole matter is in that word, "Master." What shall we call Him? Christ—the Anointed One, of whom all the prophets spoke? Jesus—called so because He should save His people from their sins? Yes; but above all, Lord. Our Lord Jesus Christ. "You call Me Master and Lord; and you say well, for so I am."

DAY 65
Fishers of Men: Part 2 of 3
by David James Burrell

(Excerpted from *The Golden Passion*, published by Wilbur B. Ketcham, New York, New York in 1897)

"Do not be afraid; from now on you will be catching men."
Luke 5:10

It is remarkable, when we stop to reflect, that these men should have responded to the Master's words, "Launch out into the deep and let down your nets." Who is this Man, so ready with His counsel? They knew all about the business of fishing. They were born here at Gennesaret. They had floated their toy boats along the edge of the water and fished with crooked pins when they were lads. They knew the haunts and habits of all the fish. They knew the weather signs. They could call the name of every wind that blew across the waters. And who is this that offers advice? A carpenter of Nazareth. He had served His apprenticeship with saw and plane; He knew how to mend plows and furniture, but what did He know about fishing?

Ah, but He was their Master. That tells the story. There was no reservation in their submission to Him. Their acquaintance with this man was but slight as yet; they had met Him at the banks of the Jordan, when the prophet of the wilderness said, "Behold the Lamb of God!" But they were ready to accept His counsel in temporal things as well as in spiritual things. There was no questioning, no hesitation, no reserve. We know more of Jesus than they did. We have a deeper personal experience of His power to save. We have seen Him controlling the affairs of people and nations—the commanding figure in the history of these nineteen centuries. If John and Peter and James could say, "Master, Your word is ultimate," how much more should we!

His mastery is over every department of life. His counsel is for the marketplace as well as the sanctuary. These are troublesome times in the business world; people are worrying all day, and passing sleepless nights. Are you, my friend, in financial trouble? Go to your Master with it. Is He not the silent partner in your affairs? He knows all, is interested in all that concerns you. It was for people under such circumstances that He spoke this word: "Consider the ravens; for they neither sow nor reap; they have neither storehouse nor barn; and God feeds them; how much more valuable are you than they are?"

He is Master, also, with reference to the duties of the religious life. You are a member of the great fellowship; you have entered into a covenant with Him in the service of the kingdom of God; you want to know what to do. "I am a fisher of men, but where shall I cast the net?" Ask and He will direct you. The beginning of all spiritual usefulness is in the word of Paul: "Lord, what will You have me do?"

***

"And whatsoever He says unto you, do it." Do it at any cost of personal convenience. Do it, however His counsel may seem to conflict with your own ideas of common sense and respectability. Do it without delay or questioning. Do it because He is Master and His word is ultimate. The best offering that a person can make to their Lord is absolute obedience. All the trophies of wealth and honor that the most distinguished of mortals may bring cannot supply the lack of it. The best of the animals fattened for slaughter, with King Agag in bonds, could not prevent the prophet's word, "To obey is better than sacrifice." Therefore, having submitted your life to the Master, whatever He says unto you, do it.

***

DAY 66
Fishers of Men: Part 3 of 3
by David James Burrell
(Excerpted from *The Golden Passion*, published by Wilbur B. Ketcham, New York, New York in 1897)

"Do not be afraid; from now on you will be catching men."
Luke 5:10

We sometimes think of heaven as the reward of service; but this is not so. It is indeed our El Dorado. When Godfrey [of Bouillon of France], having brought his crusaders through storms and scorching suns finally saw in the distance the glowing domes of Jerusalem, he turned to his men with this exclamation, "Who will not fight for such a city!" But heaven is not to be had for effort. Heaven is of grace. The qualifications for entering that city are, on the one hand, pardon through the blood, and on the other, sanctification by the Spirit. And pardon and sanctification are both of grace.

What then is the reward of service? Fruitfulness. The farmer is patient in scattering the seed, because he foresees the golden fields and hears the creaking of the loaded wagons. It was a right prayer that Moses made: "Let Your work appear unto Your servants, and Your glory to their children. And let the beauty of the Lord our God be upon us; and establish the work of our hands for us; yes, establish the work of our hands."

But oh, for the discouraged ones! How many there are who say like these weary fishermen, "We have worked all night and taken nothing." It is the cry that goes up from the prayer closets where parents have been pleading for the wandering children these many years. It is the prayer of the missionary who works alone in the regions of darkness and the shadow of death. [William] Carey and [Robert] Morrison, Allen Gardiner and Adoniram Judson—they dragged their nets year after year in vain. It is not work that tries the soul, but work without fruit.

What do we need? Patience? Yes, truly; but faith above all. Faith is the mother of patience. "He that believes, shall not make haste." It was faith that said, "Nevertheless, at your word I will let down the net." We can afford to wait, so long as we believe…The kingdom of heaven comes not with observation. The mustard seed grows in the night. Work on and trust God. In due time we shall reap, if we do not faint…

We live in the midst of marvels. Every throb of our pulse is a miracle; every breath we draw is a miracle. All blessings are special. It is as easy for God to turn a snowflake from its course as for the sun to stand still on Gibeon. Nothing is too hard for Him. But the wonder of the miracle in the case of Peter was its revelation of God. He saw in this Jesus of Nazareth an unveiling of the mighty God. At the same instant he saw himself a sinner. And between him and that Incarnate God a gulf opened that seemed vast and bridgeless. A moment later Jesus stretched His hand over that separating gulf and drew Peter toward Him, saying, "Fear not." He drew him into fellowship, friendship, partnership with Himself, in the things of the kingdom of God—"I will make you a fisher of men."

This was but a prophetic profile of Pentecost. On that memorable day these fishermen again let down their nets, and when they drew them in they caught three thousand souls for God. Again they were amazed. The glowing flames rested upon their brows. The miracle was accomplished which is achieved again and again in every outpouring of the Spirit of God. The Master is not far from any one of us. He is here as surely as He stood with the disciples in the little boat that day. "Follow Me," is His word, "and I will make you fishers of men."…"He that goes out and weeps, bearing precious seed, shall *doubtless, doubtless, doubtless,* come again with rejoicing, bringing his harvest with him."

DAY 67
The Disciple's Sacrifice: Part 1 of 4
by John Henry Jowett
(Excerpted from *The Passion for Souls*, published by Fleming H. Revell Company,
New York, New York in 1905)

*Now I rejoice in my sufferings for your sake, and in my flesh I am filling up
what is lacking in Christ's afflictions for the sake
of His body, that is, the church...*
Colossians 1:24

***

The gospel of a broken heart demands the ministry of bleeding hearts. If that succession is broken we lose our fellowship with the King. As soon as we cease to bleed we cease to bless. When our sympathy loses its pain we can no longer be the servants of the passion. We are no longer "filling up what is lacking in Christ's afflictions," and not to be "filling up" is to paralyze, and to "make the cross of Christ ineffective." Now the apostle was a man of the most vivid and realistic empathy. "Who is weak and I am not weak?" [2 Corinthians 11:29]. His empathy was a perpetuation of the Passion. I am amazed at its intensity and scope. What a broad, exquisite surface of perceptiveness he exposed to the needs and sorrows of the race! Wherever there was a pain it tore the strings of his sensitive heart. Now it is the painful fears and alarms of a runaway slave, and now the dumb, dark agonies of people far away.

The apostle felt as vividly as he thought, and he lived through all he saw. He was being continually aroused by the sighs and cries of his fellow men. He heard a cry from Macedonia, and the pain on the distant shore was reflected in his own life. That is the only recorded voice, but he was hearing them every day, wandering, pain-filled, fear-filled voices, calling out of the night, voices from Corinth, from Athens, from Rome also, and from distant Spain! "Who is weak and

I am not weak?" He was exhausted with other folk's exhaustion, and in the heavy weight of burdens he touched the mystery of Gethsemane, and had fellowship with the sufferings of his Lord.

My brothers and sisters, are we in this succession? Does the cry of the world's need pierce the heart and ring even through the fabric of our dreams? Are we "filling up" our Lord's sufferings with our own sufferings, or are we the unsympathetic ministers of a mighty Passion?

I am amazed how easily I become callous. I am ashamed how small and insensitive is the surface which I present to the needs and sorrows of the world. I so easily become wrapped up in the soft cloth of self-indulgence, and the cries from far and near cannot reach my comfortable soul.

"Why do you wish to return?" I asked a noble young missionary who had been sent home due to illness: "Why do you wish to return?" "Because I can't sleep for thinking of them!"

But, my brethren, except when I spend a day with my Lord, the trend of my life is quite another way. I cannot think about them because I am so inclined to sleep! A numbness settles down upon my spirit, and the pains of the world awake no corresponding empathy. I can read my newspaper, which is oftentimes a veritable cupful of horrors, and I can review it at the breakfast table, and it does not add a single flavor to my feast. I wonder if one who is so unmoved can ever be a servant of the suffering Lord!

DAY 68
The Disciple's Sacrifice: Part 2 of 4
by John Henry Jowett
(Excerpted from *The Passion for Souls*, published by Fleming H. Revell Company,
New York, New York in 1905)

Now I rejoice in my sufferings for your sake, and in my flesh I am filling up
what is lacking in Christ's afflictions for the sake
of His body, that is, the church...
Colossians 1:24

Here in my newspaper is the long, small-typed casualty list from the place of war; or there is half a column of the crimes and misdemeanors of my city; or here are a couple of columns describing the hot and frantic events of the racecourse; or there is a small corner paragraph telling me about some massacres in China; or here are two little hidden lines saying that a man named James Chalmers has been murdered in New Guinea! And I can read it all while I eat my breakfast, and the dark record does not haunt my day with the mingled wails of the orphaned and the damned. My brethren, I do not know how any Christian service is to be fruitful if the servant is not primarily baptized in the spirit of a suffering compassion. We can never heal the needs we do not feel. Tearless hearts can never be the heralds of the Passion. We must pity if we would redeem. We must bleed if we would be the ministers of the saving blood. We must complete by our passion the Passion of the Lord, and by our own suffering sympathies we must be "filling up what is lacking in Christ's afflictions." "Put on, therefore, as the elect of God" a heart of compassion [Colossians 3:12-14].

Here is another association: Can we find a vital kinship? "He offered up prayers and supplications with strong crying and tears" [Hebrews 5:7]. So far the Master. "I would have you know how greatly I agonize for you" [Colossians 2:1]. So far the Apostle Paul. The

Savior prayed "with strong crying and tears"; His apostle "agonized" in intercession! Is the association legitimate? Did not the agony at Rome take care of "filling up" the "strong cryings" at Jerusalem? Does not the interceding apostle enter into the fellowship of his Master's sufferings, and complete that "what is lacking"? The intercession in Rome is related to the intercession in Jerusalem, and both are affairs of blood.

If the prayer of the disciple is to be "filling up" the intercession of the Master, the disciple's prayer must be troubled with much crying and many tears. The ministers of Calvary must plead in bloody sweat, and their intercession must often touch the point of agony. If we pray in cold blood we are no longer ministers of the Cross.

True intercession is a sacrifice, a bleeding sacrifice, a perpetuation of Calvary, a "filling up" of the sufferings of Christ. St. Catherine told a friend that the anguish which she experienced, in the realization of the sufferings of Christ, was greatest at the moment when she was pleading for the salvation of others. "Promise me that You will save them!" she cried, and stretching out her right hand to Jesus, she again implored in agony, "Promise me, dear Lord, that You will save them. O give me a token that You will." Then her Lord seemed to clasp her outstretched hand in His, and to give her the promise, and she felt a piercing pain as though a nail had been driven through the palm.

I think I know the meaning of the mystic experience. She had become so absolutely one with the interceding Savior that she entered into the fellowship of His crucifixion. Her prayers were red with sacrifice, and she felt the grasp of the pierced hand.

DAY 69
The Disciple's Sacrifice: Part 3 of 4
by John Henry Jowett
(Excerpted from *The Passion for Souls*, published by Fleming H. Revell Company,
New York, New York in 1905)

Now I rejoice in my sufferings for your sake, and in my flesh I am filling up
what is lacking in Christ's afflictions for the sake
of His body, that is, the church…
Colossians 1:24

"Master, the Jews of late sought to stone You, and You go out there again?" [John 11:8]. "Having stoned Paul" [at Lystra] "they drew him out of the city supposing he had been dead." And Paul "returned again to Lystra!" [Acts 14:19, 21]. Back to the stones! Is that in the succession? Is not the apostle the counterpart of his Master? Is he not doing in Lystra what his Master did in Judaea? Is he not filling up "what is lacking in Christ's afflictions"? Back to the stones! "Master, the Jews of late sought to stone You, and You go out there again?" The Boxers [in China] of late sought to decimate you, poor little flock, and you go out there again? The New Guineans have butchered your [James] Chalmers and your [Oliver] Tompkins, and you go out there again? Mongolia has swallowed your people and your treasure, and its prejudice and its suspicions appear unmoved, and you go out there? You have been tiring yourself for years, seeking to redeem this person and that person, and who treats you with indifference and contempt, and you go out there again?

My brethren, are we familiar with the road that leads back to the stones? It was familiar to the Apostle Paul, and when he trod the heavy way he entered the fellowship of his Master's pains, and knew "what is lacking in Christ's afflictions" of his Lord. To go again and face the stones is to perpetuate the spirit of the Man who "set His face steadfastly to go to Jerusalem" [Luke 9:51] even though it meant derision, desertion, and the Cross.

We never really know our Master until we kneel and labor among the forceful stones. Only as we experience the "fellowship of His sufferings can we know the power of His resurrection." There is a sentence in David Hill's biography—that rare, gentle, refined spirit, who moved like a fragrance in his little part of China—a sentence which has burned itself into the very marrow of my mind. Disorder had broken out, and one of the rioters seized a huge splinter of a smashed door and gave him a terrific blow on the wrist, almost breaking his arm. And how is it all referred to? "There is a deep joy in actually suffering physical violence for Christ's sake." That is all! It is a strange combination of words—suffering, violence, joy! And yet I remember the message of the apostle, "If we suffer with Him we shall also reign with Him" [Romans 8:17] and I cannot forget that the epistle which has much to say about tribulation and loss, has most to say about rejoicing! "As the sufferings of Christ abound in us, so our consolation also abounds through Christ" [2 Corinthians 1:5]…

These men did not shrink from the labor when the stones began to fly. Rejection was an invitation to return! The strength of opposition acted upon them like an inspiration. Have you ever noticed that magnificent turn which the apostle gives to a certain passage in his first letter to the Corinthians [16:8-9]? "I will tarry at Ephesus…for a great door and effectiveness is opened unto me, and there are many adversaries"! "There are many adversaries…I will tarry"! The majestic opposition constitutes a reason to remain! "There are many adversaries"; I will hold on!

My brethren, that is the martyr's road, and one who treads that way lives the martyr's life, and even though he or she does not die the martyr's death, he or she shall have the martyr's crown. Back to the stones! "It is the way the Master went," and to be found in that way is to perpetuate the sacrificial spirit, and to be "filling up what is lacking in Christ's afflictions."

DAY 70
The Disciple's Sacrifice: Part 4 of 4
by John Henry Jowett
(Excerpted from *The Passion for Souls*, published by Fleming H. Revell Company,
New York, New York in 1905)

*Now I rejoice in my sufferings for your sake, and in my flesh I am filling up
what is lacking in Christ's afflictions for the sake
of His body, that is, the church…*
Colossians 1:24

To be, therefore, in the sacrificial succession, our sympathy must be
a passion, our intercession must be a groaning, our giving must be a
sacrifice, and our service must be a martyrdom. In everything there
must be the "shedding of blood." How can we achieve it? What is
the secret of the sacrificial life? It is here. The men and the women
who willingly and joyfully share the fellowship of Christ's sufferings
are vividly conscious of the unspeakable reality of their own
personal redemption. They never forget the pit out of which they
have been lifted, and they never lose the memory of the grace that
saved them. "He loved me, and gave Himself for me" [Galatians
2:20]; *therefore*, "I glory in tribulation!" [Romans 5:3]. "By the grace
of God I am what I am" [1 Corinthians 15:10]; *therefore* "I will very
gladly spend and be spent!" [2 Corinthians 12:15]. The insertion of
the "therefore" is not illegitimate: it is the implied conjunction
which reveals the secret of the sacrificial life.

When Henry Martyn reached the shores of India he made this entry
in his journal, "I desire to burn out for my God," and at the end of
the far-off years the secret of his grand enthusiasm stood openly
revealed. "Look at me," he said to those about him as he was dying,
"Look at me, the vilest of sinners, but saved by grace! Amazing that
I can be saved!" It was that amazement, wondering all through his

years, that made him such a fountain of sacrificial energy in the service of his Lord.

My brethren, are we in the succession? Are we "shedding our blood"? Are we "filling up what is lacking in Christ's afflictions"? They are doing it among the heathen. It was done in Uganda, when that handful of lads, having been tortured, and their arms cut off, and while they were being slowly burned to death, raised a song of triumph, and praised their Savior in the fire, "singing until their shriveled tongues refused to form the sound." They are doing it in China, the little remnant of the decimated churches gathering here and there upon the very spots of butchery and martyrdom, and renewing their covenant with the Lord. They are "filling up that which is behind of the sufferings of Christ."

They are doing it among the missionaries. James Hannington was doing it when he wrote this splendidly heroic word, when he encountered tremendous opposition: "I refuse to be disappointed; I will only praise!" James Chalmers was doing it when, after long years of hardship and difficulty, he proclaimed his unalterable choice: "Recall the twenty-one years, give me back all its experience, give me its shipwrecks, give me its standings in the face of death, give it back to me surrounded with savages with spears and clubs, give it me back again with spears flying about me, with the club knocking me to the ground—give it back to me, and I will still be your missionary!" Are *we* in the succession?

> "A noble army, men and boys,
> The matron and the maid,
> Around the Savior's throne rejoice,
> In robes of light arrayed;
> They climbed the steep ascent of Heaven
> Through peril, toil and pain!
> O God, to us may grace be given
> To follow in their train."

DAY 71
The Holy Spirit's Present Help in Missions: Part 1 of 7
by Adoniram Judson (A. J.) Gordon
(Excerpted from *The Holy Spirit in Missions*, published by Fleming H. Revell Company,
New York, New York in 1893)

As imperatively as you will need the Holy Spirit *in* the work, not less imperatively do you need Him to equip you *for* the work. What we call sacred learning constantly tends to become secular, because of the absence of daily dependence upon the illuminating and sanctifying Spirit. I do not know that the study of Hebrew or of theology is any more divine in itself than the study of mathematics. I go further and affirm what the history of the Church is constantly proving, that the pursuit of these studies without a humble and prayerful dependence on God may be absolutely injurious to one's Christian life.

Professor Beck of Tubingen uttered a bold but true remark when he said to his class one day: "Gentlemen, remember that without the illumination of the Spirit, theology is not only a cold stone, it is a deadly poison." You can verify this saying by asking and answering the question: From where comes the most subtle and dangerous form of unbelief which we are encountering at the present time? Does it not come from the theological chairs in Germany, in Holland, and elsewhere, which have been founded to instruct young men in the principles of our divine religion?...The Holy Scriptures, literally inspired and doctrinally infallible—these are the foundations on which the Protestant Church has been taught to rest for her faith, for her life, for her hope. And who is it that is doing most to unsettle those foundations today? Not the illiterate layperson of our churches, whose misfortune is that they have never studied Hebrew or mastered theology; nor the brilliant and cultured opponents of Christianity—the skeptics and agnostics and theists; but the ones whose office is to teach Hebrew and theology, and to instruct our young people in the doctrines and principles of the gospel of Christ. And these are leading astray, I believe, principally because they suppose that the Bible can be understood by microscopic interpretation and by philosophical analysis, when the Book itself repeatedly declares the contrary. "For what man knows the things of a man, except the spirit of man which is in him?" asks the apostle; "even so the things of God knows no man, but the Spirit of God" [1 Corinthians 2:11]. There is a finer sense than the scientific; there is a more delicate touch than the interpretive. It is written, and cannot be altered: "The natural man receives not the things of the Spirit of God, for they are foolishness unto him; neither can he know them, because they are spiritually discerned" [1 Corinthians 2:14].

The Bible is burglar-proof against all unsanctified learning. It repeatedly suffers violence at the hands of scholars, and the violent seek to take it by force. But the Holy Spirit alone holds the key to it. He alone knows the combination of faith and study by which it can be unlocked and all its hidden treasures of wisdom and knowledge appropriated. It was a very notable utterance that a French preacher expressed when he exclaimed, "My brethren, we have unlearned the Holy Spirit." Not to know is one thing; to not know that which we have once learned is quite another thing. If through a growing pride of culture we gradually outgrow that childlike trust in the guidance and illumination of the Spirit which we once enjoyed, what is our learning but a deplorable unlearning?...To modify a famous phrase of Augustine, I would affirm that "the sufficiency of our learning is to discover that our learning is insufficient." The great teacher is now the Holy Ghost...He has come to take His place in the Church. Our glorified Lord entrusted us with His teaching, saying, "He that has an ear let him hear what the Spirit says unto the churches" [Revelation 2:17]. You are bound to give the highest respect to your theological instructors; but it is also your most solemn duty to have the Holy Spirit as your private Tutor—in your prayer closet, in your classroom, and ultimately in your ministry, to have Him for your personal instructor; for He offers Himself to be that for you.

The Holy Spirit's Present Help in Missions: Part 2 of 7

by Adoniram Judson (A. J.) Gordon

(Excerpted from *The Holy Spirit in Missions*, published by Fleming H. Revell Company,
New York, New York in 1893)

We talk much of the baptism of the Spirit, the anointing of the Spirit, and the infusing of the Spirit, meaning thereby something above and beyond what we received in conversion. I cannot emphasize too strongly the importance of this transaction. And yet I want to avoid perplexing you by causing you to strive after some stereotyped experience of the Spirit's anointing. I remember that it was a great discovery in my own study of redemption when I learned that justification comes not so much through Christ's doing some new thing for us, as by our realizing and taking hold, through faith, that which He has already done. So does the Holy Spirit. The promise of His coming and indwelling in the Church has been fulfilled: "If I go away, I will send you another Comforter" [John 16:7], Advocate, Helper, Teacher. If we consciously and believingly surrender to the Holy Spirit, and accept Him implicitly in all these roles, this is the infusing of power. Attach the train to the locomotive and immediately all the power and speed which belongs to the engine is linked to the cars; and so the energy of the Holy Ghost is ours in proportion as we surrender to Him and attach ourselves to Him.

An eminent teacher of theology, Principal [Handley] Moule of Cambridge, England, in his admirable work on the Holy Spirit, describes his own experience this way: "Never shall I forget the gain to conscious faith and peace which came to my own soul, not long after a first decisive and taking hold of the crucified Lord as the sinner's sacrifice of peace, from a more intelligent and conscious hold upon the living and most gracious personality of that Holy Spirit through whose mercy the soul had got that blessed view. It was a new development of insight into the love of God. It was a new contact, as it were, with the inner and eternal movements of redeeming goodness and power, a new discovery in divine resources."

This "new discovery of divine resources" is what I would instruct you to seek. "The promise of the Father" of which Jesus spoke has been fulfilled. The Holy Ghost has been given. And now the question which I would urge upon you is that which Paul put to certain Ephesian Christians: "Have you received the Holy Ghost since you believed?" [Acts 19:2]. Have you solemnly and definitely surrendered to His guidance? Have you consciously taken hold of Him as your supreme dependence for strength and service? If you have, you have discovered the secret of power, and that power will become more and more real to you every day you live. How imperatively do you need this infusing of the Spirit to equip you for your work as missionaries of the cross!

More than a hundred years ago a young missionary lay dying at thirty-eight years of age. David Brainerd, who passed away from earth at the house of Jonathan Edwards in Northampton, on October 9, 1747, was one of the holiest men and one of the most remarkable missionaries who has appeared in any age of the Church. One of his last recorded prayers was "for the influences of the divine Spirit to descend on ministers in a special manner." His dying counsel to his brother, whom he desired to succeed him, was "to strive to obtain much of the grace of God's Spirit in the heart," significantly adding, "When ministers feel the special gracious influences of the Holy Spirit in their hearts, it wonderfully assists them to come at the consciences of people, and, as it were, to handle them; whereas without these, whatever reason or oratory we may employ, we do but make use of stumps instead of hands."

The Holy Spirit's Present Help in Missions: Part 3 of 7
by Adoniram Judson (A. J.) Gordon
(Excerpted from *The Holy Spirit in Missions*, published by Fleming H. Revell Company, New York, New York in 1893)

I know of nothing more nearly resembling Pentecost than the scenes which followed David Brainerd's preaching at Crossweeksung, New Jersey. Even he himself looked on with astonishment and awe at the power of the gospel on the hearts of the Indians [Native Americans]. But the secret is clear when we look from the field to the prayer closet and see him praying whole days for the anointing of the Holy Ghost to come upon him; and praying with such intensity that his garments were wet with the sweat of his intercession. What an example for us to set constantly before us! And now that he had been heard, he could grasp the hearts of these unresponsive Indians, not with the "stumps" of reason and logic, but with the invisible and irresistible fingers of the Holy Spirit. What an incalculable difference it makes when either we preach the gospel in the energy of the flesh or in the might of the Spirit!

Peter, who had witnessed the marvelous scenes of Pentecost, had only this single explanation of the results, when afterwards referring to them: "We have preached the gospel unto you with the Holy Ghost sent down from heaven" [1 Peter 1:12]. It costs much to obtain the power of the Spirit: it costs self-surrender and being humbled and the yielding up of our most precious things to God; it costs the perseverance of long waiting, and the faith of strong trust. But when we are really in that power we shall find this difference: that whereas before it was hard for us to do the easiest things, now it is easy for us to do the hardest things.

James Hervey, the friend of [John] Wesley at Oxford, describes the change which took place in him through his anointing by the Spirit:

that while his preaching was once like the firing of an arrow, all the speed and force thereof depending on the strength of his arm in bending the bow, now it was like the firing of a rifle-ball, the whole force depending on the powder, and needing only a finger-touch to set it off. O Holy Spirit, come upon us in Your fullness, and teach us this secret of the irresistible might of weakness—of doing great things for God through the energy of that Spirit by whom God does great things for us!

The missionary especially needs the indwelling of the Spirit to enable them to reproduce the life of Christ in the middle of the heathen. "Be not conformed to this world, but be transformed by the renewing of your minds" [Romans 12:2], is the great word of the apostle. And this must be accomplished by inward transformation, and not by outward imitation. It is only the Spirit of the Lord within us that can reproduce the image of God set before us. This image, literally manifested, is the most powerful of all sermons for impressing the heathen.

An intelligent and respected Hindu, Surendra Nath Banerjya, in addressing a company of students not long ago in Calcutta, said: "What India needs for her regeneration is not simply sermons and speeches and Bible texts, but the presentation of a truly Christian life, the gentleness and meekness and forgiveness such as your Christ exhibited in His life and death." Undoubtedly this is true, and of the signs and wonders and gifts of the Holy Ghost which God has promised to accompany the preaching of His Word among the heathen, none is greater than this. I do not refer simply to an exhibition of the agreeable virtues of Jesus Christ, but to a literal conformity to His life of poverty and suffering and self-denial for the good of others.

DAY 74
The Holy Spirit's Present Help in Missions: Part 4 of 7
by Adoniram Judson (A. J.) Gordon

(Excerpted from *The Holy Spirit in Missions*, published by Fleming H. Revell Company, New York, New York in 1893)

The impression made by Christian Frederick Schwartz upon the people of India is to this day spoken of by missionary historians with a kind of suppressed astonishment. Among the lower classes his influence was apostolic [like the influence of the Apostles]; with the upper classes it was almost imperial. Yet he did not win people from a palace. On the contrary, he lived in a single room just large enough to hold himself and his bed, existing on rice and vegetables cooked in native fashion, his entire support costing less than two hundred and fifty dollars annually. By this humbling to people of low status, he won people of all ranks as few others have ever done in the history of the Church. A remarkable life lived in our own time—that of George Bowen of Bombay—provides perhaps the nearest likeness to that of Schwartz. He repeated the Savior's self-denial without falling into the monk's austerity, so that Dr. William Hanna of Scotland speaks of him as "one who exhibited a degree of self-sacrificing devotion to which there is perhaps no existing parallel in the whole field of missionary labor." The influence which he exerted and the reverence which he inspired were equal to his devotion. It will take many years to obliterate from India the memory of either.

Such also was William C. Burns of China. He traveled, like his Master, from city to city, accepting such hospitalities as the people might offer, content with the pilgrim's portion, the plainest food and clothing, and enduring for Christ's sake with the utmost meekness every indignity laid upon him. We are not surprised to find his biographer declaring that the impression of his words on the people of China was insignificant in comparison with that of his

Christ-like life. So it always is. The person is greater than the sermon. Translators are always needed on heathen fields; but the greatest among them is the one who can translate the example of Jesus Christ into the dialect of daily life, into the universal speech of pain and poverty and suffering for the sake of others.

Anskar, a missionary to the Scandinavians in the ninth century, when asked by his heathen listeners whether he could perform miracles, replied with noble wisdom: "If God were indeed to grant that power to me, I would only ask that I might exhibit the miracle of a holy life." The evidential character of such a miracle is perhaps even greater than those formed on external nature; for it touches the heart by its brotherly appeal instead of staggering the intellect by its supernatural mystery. Surely it is a prayer worthy of being offered daily, that the Holy Spirit will work in us and exhibit through us the miracle of a Christ-like life.

We should make very practical for the actual, daily experience of missionary life all that we are saying concerning the power and blessing of the Holy Spirit. Why not rely upon this divine Executor of missions with a hundred times more confidence than we extend to any person or to any group of people? Once at least are we implored by "the love of the Spirit" in the exhortations of Scripture. It is a comforting and uplifting expression. Our Almighty Helper has such affection towards those who are striving to fulfill their Lord's commission that He will be most ready in His assistance when they need Him most in their weakness.

DAY 75
The Holy Spirit's Present Help in Missions: Part 5 of 7
by Adoniram Judson (A. J.) Gordon
(Excerpted from *The Holy Spirit in Missions*, published by Fleming H. Revell Company,
New York, New York in 1893)

The following glimpse into the inner life of a missionary church is more instructive and cheering than any formal exhortations which we can make about the importance of repeatedly seeking the filling of the Spirit. It is from a report by Dr. Griffith John of Hankow, China. He says:

> Feeling my lack of spiritual power, I spent the whole of Saturday in an earnest prayer for a baptism of the Holy Ghost. On the following morning I preached on the subject. At the close of the service I proposed that we should meet for an hour every day of the following week to pray for a baptism of the Holy Ghost. From fifty to seventy of the converts met day by day, and confessing their sins pleaded with tears for an outpouring of the Spirit of God. The native Church at Hankow received an impulse the force of which continues to this day. The Holy Ghost became a mighty reality to many. Where once other things were preached, Christ and His power became a living reality.

The Church is not merely a voluntary association of believers. It is the body of the Holy Ghost, the "habitation of God through the Spirit." Why, then, when it is faint or declining, should our immediate impulse not be to seek a renewal of the Spirit's indwelling life? Shall the exhausted missionaries in the tropics move to higher altitudes for the reinvigorating atmosphere, and not with far more eagerness seek to enter into the freer air of the Spirit, when their inward strength has become weakened? No, why not strive to make our communion with the Spirit so habitual that we shall never become exhausted? This is but the same exhortation in another form with which the Scripture presents us: "If we live in the Spirit, let us walk in the Spirit" [Galatians 5:25]. The divine provision and intention is for His perpetual indwelling. "In the old dispensation, the Spirit worked upon believers, but He did not in His person dwell in believers. Engaged to the soul, the Spirit went often to see His betrothed, but was not yet one with her; the marriage was not consummated until Pentecost, after the glorification of Jesus Christ. Then was Christ's word fulfilled: He shall be in you" [G. F. Tophel]…

It is the indwelling of the Holy Spirit, given to Christ's servants for sustaining them in their labors and discouragements. The Holy Ghost is omnipresence [everywhere] in the great body of Christ; and omniscient [all-knowing] in His oversight of the vast work of that body in evangelizing the world. It is because the individual disciple can take in so little of the complete arrangement that he is so exposed to discouragement. The thwarting of well-planned missionary endeavors; the removal from the field of devoted laborers, and the death of others before their work has been fairly begun—these are circumstances which often perplex and confuse the thoughtful missionary. Has He who commands His servants to go into all the world and preach the gospel to every creature no oversight of His work, no protection over His workers, that going in implicit obedience to His word they are still without a guarantee of divine preservation and support? Who knows the inner, unwritten, tearful book of questionings on this theme which has been written in many a missionary's heart! But the great brooding, over-watching Spirit abides in the Church to solve all these difficulties and to silence all these doubts. He alone sees the relationship of present loss to future gain; of suffering for Christ now to the glory that shall follow; and the final overbalance of present light afflictions by the "far more exceeding and eternal weight of glory" [2 Corinthians 4:17]. And knowing all, He alone can strengthen us to labor "in the kingdom and patience of Jesus Christ" [Revelation 1:9].

DAY 76
The Holy Spirit's Present Help in Missions: Part 6 of 7
by Adoniram Judson (A. J.) Gordon
(Excerpted from *The Holy Spirit in Missions*, published by Fleming H. Revell Company,
New York, New York in 1893)

Of how many modern heroes of the gospel may it be said, as of the ancient ones, "These all died in the faith, not having received the promises, but having seen them afar off, and were persuaded by them, and embraced them" [Hebrews 11:13]...

Allen Gardiner, upon his third heroic but futile attempt to plant the gospel in Tierra del Fuego [Argentina], dies of slow starvation; yet he writes as his last testimony: "I neither hunger nor thirst, though five days without food. Marvelous loving-kindness to me, a sinner!" The young and accomplished Bishop John Coleridge Patteson, cruising among the New Hebrides and telling from island to island the story of Jesus, comes at last to Nukapu, where he tells to the natives on the shore the story of the martyrdom of Stephen; when, without warning, he is suddenly slain, and, like his Master, sent back with five ghastly wounds upon his person, inflicted by the hands of those to whom he had gone preaching peace. And yet they that looked upon his dead face declared that it seemed "as it had been the face of an angel." That gifted young missionary martyr, Bishop James Hannington, dying at Uganda amid every degradation and cruelty which African savagery could inflict, is yet filled with such love and faith for his enemies that he said to his executioners: "Go tell [Chief] Mwanga that I die for Baganda, and that I have purchased the road to Uganda with my life." Such was his word to his enemies; and to his friends his farewell message was: "If this is the last chapter of my earthly history, then the next will be the first page of the heavenly—no blots, no blemishes, no incoherence, but sweet conversation in the presence of the Lamb."

How long is the list of such untimely deaths on the missionary field! And how rich and moving the dying confessions gathered from there. "Though a thousand fall, let not Africa be forgotten!" is the last plea of the young and ardent Melville Cox, falling on the field of the Dark Continent almost as soon as he had put his hand to the plow. And the lovely, sweet-faced boy, as he seems to us as we gaze upon his picture—Adam McAll—stricken down with fatal disease before his work on the Congo was barely begun, and yet breathing out as his dying prayer: "Lord, You know that I consecrated my life to preaching the gospel in Africa. If You do take me now instead of the work which I intended to give You, what is that to me? Your will be done."

And what shall we say of such untimely removals of the most devoted and useful servants from their work? We can say nothing; but the Holy Ghost witnesses: "Yes, says the Spirit, for they rest from their labors, and their works do follow them" [Revelation 13:14]. As sure as the ordinances of heaven this is true. Adalbert [of Prague], a missionary to the Wends of Prussia in the tenth century, went out singing to meet the infuriated savages, and crying in pleading tones: "For your salvation I am come, that forsaking your mute idols you may believe in the one true God, and believing in His name you may have eternal life." But like those noble bishops whom we have just mentioned, his message of love was met by the weapons of murder. Pierced by the lances of the pagans, he stretched forth both his hands, and saying, "Jesus, receive Thou me," he fell, with his face to the ground, in the form of a crucifix, thereby, as [Thomas] Carlyle says, "signing that heathen country with the sign of the cross." The martyr's mortgage then placed upon the land has long since been redeemed, and the nation has become Christian. So it ever has been, so it ever will be, when time enough has elapsed for God to fulfill His far-reaching purposes. And it is the work of the Holy Ghost to inspire the long patience and the confident hope which grasps and rejoices in this completion.

DAY 77
The Holy Spirit's Present Help in Missions: Part 7 of 7
by Adoniram Judson (A. J.) Gordon
(Excerpted from *The Holy Spirit in Missions*, published by Fleming H. Revell Company, New York, New York in 1893)

The last word of the Spirit on the last page of Scripture is one with which we may fittingly close this lecture: "And the Spirit and the Bride say, Come" [Revelation 22:17]. Some commentators explain this as an advent-call rather than a gospel-call; as a response to the Lord's, "Surely I come quickly" [Revelation 22:20], which has just been heard, rather than a part of the evangelical invitation, "Whoever will, let him take" [Revelation 22:17]. If this is so, what a lovely ideal is presented here of the watchful and faithful missionary Church! With eyes turned heavenward, the Bride is ever calling to the Bridegroom, "Even so, come, Lord Jesus" [Revelation 22:20], the Holy Spirit, the Friend of the Bridegroom, inspiring and sustaining this cry throughout the ages. At the same time, with hands outstretched towards a famishing world, both are calling: "And let him that hears say, Come; and let him that is thirsty come; and whoever will, let him take the water of life freely" [Revelation 22:17]. The heart of the missionary must maintain this double direction if it is to be kept from discouragement on the one hand and from dreaminess on the other. The uplifted gaze without the outstretched hands tends to make one visionary; the outstretched hands without the upward look tends to make one weary. Evermore must "the patience of hope" walk with equal footsteps with "the labor of love" until the Lord shall come.

How many of the most apostolic [apostle-like] missionaries have truly maintained this two-fold attitude! Of all the noble army of such, what more engaging figure rises before us than that of the venerable John Eliot among his "praying Indians" of New England! At eighty-five years of age his practical friends urge that it is time for him to cease from his missionary toils. His reply is, "My understanding leaves me, my strength fails me, but, thank God, my charity [love] holds out." And so he keeps his hand upon the plow, while his eyes meantime are lifted up to heaven in constant watching. "While he was therefore making his retreat out of the world," wrote Cotton Mather, "his discourses ran from time to time on the coming of the Lord Jesus Christ. It was the theme about which he still had recourse, and whatever other subject he was upon we were sure to hear something of this. On this he talked, of this he prayed, for this he longed."

Johann Ludwig Krapf, noble pioneer of African missions, dying on his knees like George Schmidt and David Livingstone before him, with the burden of the Dark Continent on his heart, departed in the same apostolic attitude: "I am so penetrated by the feeling of the nearness of the Lord's coming that I cannot describe it," he said one evening in November, 1881. "He is near indeed; oh, we ought to redeem the time, and hold ourselves in readiness, that we may be able to say with a good conscience, 'Even so, come, Lord Jesus.'" Thus he spoke, and retired to rest. Next morning they found him kneeling lifeless by his bedside. "Blessed are the dead that die in the Lord from now on, yes, said the Spirit" [Revelation 14:13]. And also He said: "Blessed are those servants whom the Lord shall find watching when He comes" [Luke 12:37].

DAY 78
From an Unpublished Report on Nigeria: Part 1 of 4
by Mary Slessor
(Excerpted from *Mary Slessor of Calabar: Pioneer Missionary* by William Pringle
Livingstone, published by George H. Doran Company,
New York, New York in 1917)

Mr. Livingstone's Introduction to Ms. Slessor's Report
Africa is slow to change: the centuries roll over it, leaving scarcely a trace of their passing; the years come and go, and the people remain the same: all effort seems in vain. Could one weak woman affect the conditions even in a small district of the mighty continent?

It had been uphill work for her. At first there had been only a resistant response to the message she brought.

When some impression had been made she found that it soon disappeared. In ordinary life the people were volatile, quick as fire to resent, and as quick to forgive and forget, and they were the same in regard to higher things. They went into rapture over the gospel, prayed aloud, clasped their hands, shed tears, and then went back to their drinking, sacrificing, and quarrelling. They kept to all the old ways in case they might miss the right one. "Yes, Ma'," they would say, "that is right for you; but you and we are different."

But she never lost hope. "There is not much progress to report," she was accustomed to say, "and yet very much to thank God for, and to lead us to take courage." She was quite content to go on bringing rays of sunshine into the dark lives of the people, and securing for the children better conditions than their fathers had. "After all," she would say, "it comes back to this: Christ sent me to preach the gospel, and He will look after results." She was always much comforted by the thought of something she had heard the Rev. Dr. Beatt, of her old church in Aberdeen [Scotland], say in a sermon: she could recall nothing but one phrase, and one of these was, "Between the sower and the reaper stands the Husbandman." But results there were of a most important kind, and it is time to take stock of them. Fortunately, she was persuaded at this time to jot down some impressions of her work, and these, which were never published, give the best idea of the remarkable change which had been accomplished in the life and habits of Okoyong [Nigeria]. It will be noticed that she does not use the pronoun "I." Whenever she gave a statement of her work she always wrote "we," as if she were a co-worker with a Higher Power.

Ms. Slessor's Unpublished Report (approximately 1895)

In these days of high pressure, people demand large profits and quick returns in every department of our commercial and national life, and these must be served up with the definiteness and precision of statistics. This abnormal and feverish haste has entered to some extent into our religious work, and is felt more or less in all the pulses of our Church. Whatever may be the reasons for such a course in regard to worldly callings, its methods and standards are utterly foreign to the laws of Christ's kingdom, and can only result in distortions and miscalculations when applied to His work. While thanking God for every evidence of life and growth, we shrink from reducing the pains of spiritual life, the development and workings of the conscience, or the impulse and trend toward God and righteousness, to any given number of figures on a table. Therefore, it is with the greatest reluctance that we endeavor to sum up some tangible proof of the power of God's Word among our heathen neighbors. While to our shame it has not been what it might and would have been, had we been more faithful and kept more in line with the will and Spirit of God, it has to the praise of the glory of His grace proved stronger than sin and Satan.

From an Unpublished Report on Nigeria: Part 2 of 4
by Mary Slessor
(Excerpted from *Mary Slessor of Calabar: Pioneer Missionary* by William Pringle
Livingstone, published by George H. Doran Company,
New York, New York in 1917)

We do not attempt to give in numbers those who are nominally Christian. Women, lads, girls, and a few men profess to have placed themselves in God's hands. All the children within reach are sent to the school without conditions. One lady of free birth and good position has borne persecution for Christ's sake. We speak with humility; for as no ordained minister has ever been resident or available for more than a short visit, no observance of the ordinances of baptism or the Lord's Supper has been held and we have not had the usual definite offers of persons as candidates for church membership. We have just kept on sowing the seed of the Word, believing that when God's time comes to gather them into the visible Church there will be some among us ready to participate in the privilege and honor.

Of results regarding the condition and conduct of our people generally, it is easier to speak. Raiding, plundering, the stealing of slaves, have almost entirely ceased. Any person from any place can come now for trade or pleasure, and stay wherever they choose, their bodies and property being as safe as in Calabar. For fully a year we have heard of nothing like violence from even the most backward of our people. They have thanked me for restraining them in the past, and begged me to be their representative, as they neither wished black man nor white man to be their king. It would be impossible, apart from a belief in God's particular and personal providence in answer to prayer, to account for the ready obedience and submission to our judgment which was given to us. It seemed sometimes to be almost miraculous that hordes of armed, drunken, passion-swayed men should pay attention and pay chivalrous homage to a woman, and one who had neither wealth nor outward display of any kind to produce the slightest sentiment in her favor. But such was the case, and we do not recollect one instance of insubordination.

As their interaction with the white people increased through trade or otherwise, they found that to submit to that authority did not mean loss of liberty but the opposite, and gradually their objections cleared away, until in 1894 they formally met and bound themselves to some extent by treaty with the Consul. Again, later, our considerate, patient, tactful Governor, Sir Claude Macdonald, met them, and at that interview the last objection was removed, and they promised unconditional surrender of the old laws which were based on unrighteousness and cruelty, and cordial acceptance of the just and, as they called it, "clean" code which he offered them in return. Since then he has proclaimed them a free people in every respect among neighboring tribes, and so, placing them on their honor, so to speak, has made out of the roughest material a lot of self-respecting people who conduct their business in a fashion from which Europeans might take lessons. Of course they need superintendence and watching, for their ideas are not so nicely balanced as ours in regard to the shades and degrees of right and wrong, but as compared with their former ideas and practice they are far away ahead of what we expected.

DAY 80
From an Unpublished Report on Nigeria: Part 3 of 4
by Mary Slessor
(Excerpted from *Mary Slessor of Calabar: Pioneer Missionary* by William Pringle
Livingstone, published by George H. Doran Company,
New York, New York in 1917)

No tribe was formerly so feared because of their utter disregard of human life, but human life is now safe. No chief ever died without the sacrifice of many lives, but this custom has now ceased. Only last month the man who, for age, wealth, and general influence exceeded all the other chiefs in Okoyong, died from the effects of cold caught three months before. We trembled, as they are at some distance from us, and every drop of European drink which could be bought from all the towns around was bought at once, and canoes were sent from every village with all the produce at command to Duke Town for some more, and all was consumed before the people dispersed from the funeral. But the only death resulting has been that of a man, who, on being blamed by the witch-doctors, went and hanged himself because the chiefs in attendance—drunk as they were—refused to give him the poison ordeal. Some chiefs, gathered for discussion at our house on the day of his death, in commenting on the wonderful change, said, "Ma, you white people are God Almighty. No other power could have done this."

With regard to infanticide and twin-murder we can speak hopefully. It will doubtless take some time to develop in them the spirit of self-sacrifice to the extent of nursing the vital spark of life for the mere love of God and humanity among the body of the people. The ideals of those emerging from heathenism are almost necessarily low. What the foreigner does is all very well for the foreigner, but the force of habit or something more subtle evidently excuses the practice of the virtue among themselves. Of course there are exceptions. All the evidence goes to show that something more tangible than sentiment or principle determines the conduct of the multitude, even among those avowedly Christian. But with all this there has dawned on them the fact that life is worth saving, even at the risk of one's own; and though chiefs and subjects alike, less than two years ago, refused to hear of the saving of twins, we have already their promise and the first instalment of their faithfulness to their promise in the persons of two baby girls, aged six and five months respectively, who have already won the hearts of some of our neighbors and the love of all the school children. Seven women have literally touched them, and all the people, including the most practical of the chiefs, come to the house and hold their discussions in full view of where the children are being nursed. One chief who, with fierce gestures, some years ago protested that we must draw the line at twins, and that they should never be brought to light in his lifetime, brought one of his children who was very ill, two months ago, and laid it on our knee alongside the twin already there, saying with a sob in his voice, "There! They are all yours, living or dying, they are all yours. Do what you like with mine."

Drinking, especially among the women, is on the decrease. The old bands of roving women who came to us at first are now only a memory and a name. The women still drink, but it is at home where the husband can keep them in check. In our immediate neighborhood it is an extremely rare thing to see a woman intoxicated, even on feast days and at funerals. None of the women who frequent our house ever taste it at all, but they still keep it for sale and give it to visitors. Indeed it is the only thing which commands a ready sale and brings ready money, and their excuse is just that of many of the church members at home, that those who want it will get it elsewhere, and perhaps in greater measure. But we have noted a decided stand being taken by several of the young mothers who have been our friends and scholars against its being given by husbands or visitors to their children...

DAY 81
From an Unpublished Report on Nigeria: Part 4 of 4
by Mary Slessor
(Excerpted from *Mary Slessor of Calabar: Pioneer Missionary* by William Pringle
Livingstone, published by George H. Doran Company,
New York, New York in 1917)

All this points to an improvement in the condition of the people generally. They are eager for education. Instead of the apathy and skeptical laugh which the mention of the Word formerly brought, the cry from all parts is for teachers; and there is a disposition to be friendly to anyone who will help them towards a higher plane of living. But it brings vividly before us the failures and weaknesses in our work; for instance, the aimlessness of our teaching, which of necessity impedes the results that under better conditions would be sure to follow. School teaching has been carried on under great difficulties owing to the scattered population, the family quarrels which made it formerly a risk to walk alone, the fear of sorcery and of the evil spirits which are supposed to dwell in the forest, the denseness of the forest itself, which makes it dangerous for children to go from one place to another without an armed escort, the withdrawing of girls when they have just been able to read in order to go to their seclusion and fattening [for marriage], and the consequent moving of them to great distances to their husbands' farms, the irregular attendance of boys who accompany their masters wherever they go, and who take the place of postmen and news-agents to the country.

There have been difficulties on our own side—the distances consume time and strength, the numerous claims made on the Mission House, the household itself which is usually a large one having, in addition to servants, those who are training for future usefulness in special spheres—as the Mission House has been until quite lately the only means of getting such training—and having usually one or more of the rescued victims of heathen customs. The pharmacy work also calls for much time and strength, nursing often having to accompany the medicine; the very ignorance and superstition of the patients and their friends making the task doubly difficult. Then one must be ever at hand to hear the complaint of and to shelter and reconcile the runaway slave or wife or the threatened victim of oppression and superstition. Visitors are to be received, and all the bothersome and, to European notions, absurd details of native etiquette are to be observed if we are to win the favor and confidence of the people.

Moreover we must be both able and willing to help ourselves in regard to the wear and tear in our dwelling and station buildings. We must make and keep in repair buildings, fences, drainage, etc., and all amid surroundings in which the climate and its forces work against us.

Add to all this the cares of housekeeping when there is no baker supply, no butcher supply, no water supply, no gas supply, no coal supply, no laundry supply, no trained-servant supply, nor untrained either for that matter, except when some native can and will lend you a slave to help you or when you can buy one—which, under ordinary circumstances is a very doubtful practice, as, though in buying the person you are literally freeing him, the natives are apt to misinterpret the motive, and unless you are very fortunate in your purchase, the slave may bring you into conflict with the powers that be, owing to their law which recognizes no freedom except that conferred by birth. After all this is seen to day by day, where is the time and strength for comprehensive and consecutive work of a more directly evangelistic and teaching type? Especially when the latter is manned year by year by the magnificent total of one individual. Is it fair to expect results under such circumstances?

[From a later letter] "But Christ is here and the Holy Spirit, and if I am seldom in a triumphant or ecstatic mood, I am always satisfied and happy in His love."

DAY 82
The Heroism of Foreign Missions: Part 1 of 3
by Phillips Brooks

(Excerpted from *The Battle of Life*, published by E. P. Dutton & Company,
New York, New York in 1910)

*While they were worshiping the Lord and fasting, the Holy Spirit said,
"Set apart for Me Barnabas and Saul for the work to which
I have called them." Then after fasting and praying they laid
their hands on them and sent them off.*
Acts 13:2-3

The work was foreign missions. The disciples in Judea were sending out two of their number to preach the gospel in other parts of Asia and, by and by, in Europe...It seems as if the arms of Christ were stretched out a little more widely. As sometimes when our Lord was preaching in the temple, those who stood nearest to Him and caught His words the freshest from His lips, those to whom His words had long been familiar, must have seen Him lift up His eyes and look across their heads to the multitude beyond who stood upon the outskirts of the crowd; and as, while they watched Him finding and speaking to those strangers, their own thoughts of Him must have enlarged; as, perhaps at first surprised and jealous, they must have come to understand Him more and love Him better for this new sight of His love for all people—so it is with us today.

Indeed there is no feeling which Jews had when they found out what had been their religion was going to become the possession of the world, which does not repeat itself now in people's minds when they hear their gospel demanding them to send it to the heathen. It must have been a surprise and bewilderment at first to find that they were not the final objects of God's care, but only the medium through which the light was to shine that it might reach other people. I can conceive that Joseph and Mary may have wondered

164

why those Gentiles should have come out of the East to worship their Messiah. But very soon the enlargement of their faith to be the world's heritage proved its power by making their faith a far holier thing for them than it could have been if it had remained wholly their own. Christ was more thoroughly theirs when through them He had been manifested to the Gentiles. And so always the enlargement of the faith brings the love of the faith, and to give the Savior to others makes Him more thoroughly our own...Let me plead for the foreign missionary idea as the necessary completion of the Christian life. It is the apex to which all the lines of the pyramid lead. The Christian life without it is a mangled and imperfect thing. The glory and the heroism of Christianity lie in its missionary life.

The departure of the disciples on their first missionary journey was a distinct epoch in the history of Christianity. There had been some anticipations of it. The gospel had been preached to the Samaritans. Philip had baptized the Ethiopian. Peter had carried his message to the Roman centurion. But now for the first time a distinct, deliberate, irrevocable step was taken, and two disciples turned their back upon the home of Judaism, which had been thus far the home of Christianity, and went out with the world before them. They went indeed in the first place to the Jews who lived in foreign lands; but when they went away from Judea they started on a work from which there was no turning back and which could not be limited. Before they had been many weeks upon their journey, it had become distinctly a mission to the Gentiles. And now, from the time when Paul and Barnabas went out on this mission, the body of the disciples divides itself into two parts. There are the disciples who stay at home and manage affairs in Jerusalem, and there are the disciples who go abroad to tell the story of the cross. Peter and James are in Jerusalem. Paul and Barnabas and Luke go wandering to Ephesus and Athens and Corinth. And, as we read our Bibles, gradually the history detaches itself from the Holy City. The interest of Christianity does not linger with the wise and faithful souls who stay at home.

DAY 83
The Heroism of Foreign Missions: Part 2 of 3
by Phillips Brooks
(Excerpted from *The Battle of Life*, published by E. P. Dutton & Company,
New York, New York in 1910)

Acts 13:2-3

Peter and James pass out of our thought. It is Paul, with his fiery zeal and eager tongue, restless to find some new ears into which to pour the story of his Master; it is he in whom the interest of Christianity is concentrated. He evidently represents its spirit. Its glory and its heroism are in him. The other disciples seem to feel this. They recognize that it is coming. They are almost like John the Baptist when he beheld Jesus. As they come down to the ship to see their companions embark, as they fast and pray and lay their hands on them and send them away, there is a seriousness about it all which is like the giving up of the most precious privilege of their work, its flower and crown, to these its missionaries; and they turn back to their administrative work at home as to a humbler and less heroic task.

The relation of the disciples who stayed at home to the disciples who went abroad to preach is the perpetual relation of the home pastor to the foreign missionary. The work of the two is not essentially different. It is essentially the same. Both have the same gospel to proclaim. But the color of their lives is different. Paul is heroic. James is unheroic, or is far less heroic. I think as we go on we will see that those words have very clear meanings. They are not vague. But even before we have defined them carefully they express a feeling with which the missionary and the pastor impress us. Heroism is in the very thought of missions. Patient devotedness, but nothing heroic, is associated with the ministry of one who works for the building up of Christian lives where Christianity already is the established faith.

I am sure that I speak for a very great many of my associates in the home ministry when I say that we feel this continually. "Sent to tell people of Christ"—that is our commission. And people certainly need to be told of Christ over and over again. Those who have known Him longest need to hear His name again and again in their temptations, their troubles, their joys. We need to tell people of Him all their lives, until we whisper His familiar name into their ears just growing dull in death. I rejoice to tell you of Him always, those of you who have heard of Him most and longest; but you can imagine, I am sure, how, standing here in your presence, and letting my thought wander off to a foreign land where some missionary is standing face to face with people who never heard of Christ before, I feel that that person is "telling people of Christ" in a more real, direct way than I am. They are coming nearer to the heart, the true idea and meaning of the work we both are doing, than I am. We are like soldiers holding the fortress. They are the soldiers who make the charge and really do the fighting.

I know the answer. I know what some of you are saying in your hearts whenever we talk together about foreign missions. "There are heathen here in Boston," you declare, "heathen enough here in America. Let us convert them first, before we go to China." That plea we all know, and I think it sounds more cheap and more shameful every year. What can be more shameful than to make the imperfection of our Christianity at home an excuse for not doing our work abroad? It is as shameless as it is shameful. It pleads for exemption and indulgence on the ground of its own neglect and sin. It is like a murderer of his father asking the judge to have pity on his orphan-hood. Even the people who make such a plea feel, I think, how unheroic it is. The minister who does what they bid him do feels his task of preaching to such people perhaps all the more necessary but certainly all the less heroic, as he sees how utterly they have failed to feel the very nature of the gospel which he preaches to them.

DAY 84
The Heroism of Foreign Missions: Part 3 of 3
by Phillips Brooks
(Excerpted from *The Battle of Life*, published by E. P. Dutton & Company,
New York, New York in 1910)

*While they were worshiping the Lord and fasting, the Holy Spirit said, "Set
apart for Me Barnabas and Saul for the work to which
I have called them." Then after fasting and praying they laid
their hands on them and sent them off.*
Acts 13:2-3

The missionary does give up his home and all the circumstances of cultivated comfortable life, and goes out across the seas, among the savages to tell them of the great Christian truth, to carry to them the gospel. I am sure that often a great deal too much has been made of the missionary's surrenders, as if they were something almost inconceivable, as if they in themselves constituted some vague sort of claim upon the respect and even the support of other people. But we are constantly reminded that that is not so. The missionaries themselves, from Paul down, have never claimed mere pity for their sacrifices.

It is other people: it is the speakers in missionary meetings who have claimed it for them. The sacrifices of the missionary every year are growing less and less. As civilization and quick communication press the globe ever smaller, and make life on the banks of the Ganges much the same that it is on the banks of the Charles River [in Boston], the sacrifices of the missionary life grow more and more slight. And always there is the fact, which people are always ready to point out, that other people do every day for gain or pleasure just what the missionary does for the gospel, and nobody wonders.

Now the missionary idea that a person is God's child gives birth to two enthusiasms: one for the Father, one for the child; one for God, one for others. The two blend together without any interference, and both together drown the missionary's self-remembrance, with all its littleness and jealousy. Who can tell, as the missionary stands there preaching the salvation to the native congregation, which fire burns the warmest in the heart? Is it love for God or for the brothers and sisters? Is it for the Master who died for the one, or for these people for whom also He died, from whom the strongest inspiration comes? No one can tell. The missionary cannot tell. The Lord Himself in His own parable foretold the noble, sweet, inextricable confusion: "Inasmuch as you have done it to one of these you have done it to Me" [Matthew 25:40]…

All that the mystic feels of personal love for God, all that the philanthropist knows of love for people, these two, each purifying and deepening and heightening the other, unite in the soul of one who goes to tell the people whom are loved as brothers and sisters, about God whom is loved as Father.

It is a little heroic even to believe in foreign missions. If we may not be among the heroes, let us, like the church of old, hear the Holy Ghost and go with Paul and Barnabas down to their ship and lay our hands on them and send them away with all our sympathy and blessing. So, perhaps, we can catch something of their heroism. So, in our quiet and home-keeping Christian lives, the idea of Christianity may become more clear, Christ our Lord more dear, and we ourselves be made more faithful, more generous, and more brave.

***

DAY 85
On Christian India: Part 1 of 3
by Henry Martyn
(Excerpted from *Sermons*, published by Crocker and Brewster,
Boston, Massachusetts in 1822)

As we have therefore opportunity, let us do good unto all men,
especially unto them who are of the household of faith.
Galatians 6:10

It is somewhat discouraging to observe how many of our best efforts for the benefit of humankind prove ineffective. Money is given away in donations, and the object of our charity is afterwards found to not have been proper; institutions are set on foot for the instruction of the poor, many of whom use their knowledge for a mischievous purpose; measures are taken for the spread of the gospel, yet many of the systems come to nothing. What then! Are we to sit still and not act until we are sure of all the success we wish for? Let us look at the farmer. The seed is scattered: some falls by the wayside, and the birds eat it; some where there is not enough earth, and when it grows up it is scorched and withers; some falls among thorns which spring up and choke it; and only a part falls onto good ground, and of that part it is but a small quantity that brings forth a hundred-fold. Yet in the hope of a harvest of some kind the farmer continues to work. So let us work, acting as best as we can judge and with all our strength because, whatever the success of our plans is in this world, we shall not lose our reward in the next. It is upon the certainty of a future reward that Paul bases the exhortation of Galatians 6:9, "in due season we shall reap if we do not quit; therefore, as we have opportunity, let us do good unto all people." This is the duty which we must first teach. Next in order, though not in importance, is the duty of paying particular attention to the household of faith...

In earthly families the father dies, and the children separate, and they are seldom pleasantly united although they live together. They neither form one body nor are energized by one spirit nor pursue the same ends nor agree in taste and inclination nor serve the same "master." But choosing each a different profession, they leave their home as fast as opportunities are made available, and eventually almost seem to forget that they ever lived under the same roof. Not so the family of faith. There is one body and one spirit, as they are called also in one hope of their calling; one Lord, one faith, one baptism, one God and Father of all, who is above all, and through all, and in them all [Ephesians 4:5-6]. Bound together by every tie, are we not affectionately exclaiming with the psalmist, "Peace be within your walls, and prosperity within your palaces. For my brethren and companions' sakes I will now say, Peace be within you" [Psalm 122:7]? We will take it for granted that this is the sentiment of your hearts. Only two things therefore remain to be considered: first, where is this family to be found? And, secondly, what can be done for them? The first question we have already answered—you need not go out of India to look for the family, for they dwell in the land, and are natives of it, and the only favor we ask for them is the gift of a Bible.

The native Christians of India may be arranged according to their languages: first—the Portuguese, of whom there are about 50,000. On the Malabar coast alone there are 36,000; at Calcutta 7,000; in Ceylon 5,000. Besides these, there are settlements of Portuguese all along the coast from Madras to Cape Comorin, and families of them are to be found in all the principal towns on the Ganges and Jumna. They are more or less mixed with the natives, and their language has in consequence lost much of its purity; but there is no reason to believe that the version of the Scriptures, in the pure Portuguese, would not be perfectly intelligible and highly acceptable to them. Copies of the Portuguese Scriptures could be acquired immediately from England, and they might be put into circulation without difficulty because here, as well as in Europe, the Roman Catholic priests no longer oppose the translation and dispersion of the Scriptures.

DAY 86
On Christian India: Part 2 of 3
by Henry Martyn
(Excerpted from *Sermons*, published by Crocker and Brewster,
Boston, Massachusetts in 1822)

Galatians 6:10

Second: The next class of Christians to be noticed are those of Tanjore who were converted to the Christian faith chiefly by the labors of [Christian Friedrich] Swartz. They number about 12,000 and speak Tamul. A version of the Scriptures in this language was made long ago by Fabricius, one of the Danish missionaries, who devoted his whole life to the work. These people are all Protestants, every one of them can read the Bible, and their desire to be more fully supplied with the Scriptures appears from a letter sent by the missionaries who oversee them. Last year these circumstances were stated to you; and with a readiness and affection which will long be remembered, you came forward at once to assist your brothers and sisters. The donations of a few individuals were sufficiently able to supply their immediate wants, but we are persuaded that still greater exertions would have been made, had the occasion required them. I am now authorized to inform you that 500 Old Testaments, 400 New, and 300 Psalters in Tamul; 200 Old Testaments, 150 New, and 500 Psalters in Portuguese have been purchased and distributed.

A new edition of the Scriptures in Tamul should be instantly prepared in order that we may be able to give them further assistance and anticipate their future wants. There are Tamul presses at Tranquebar and Vepery, and persons to operate them.

Third: then there are those who speak the Malayalim or Malabar. These are first the Roman Catholics, who number 150,000, composed partly of converts from heathenism, and partly of proselytes from the Syrian church [Orthodox]; and secondly, the Syrians who retain their ancient form of worship. No estimate has been made of their population, but the number of their churches is determined to be fifty-five. There are then, perhaps, not fewer than 200,000 Christians who use the Malabar language. A translation of the Scriptures into it was undertaken four years ago by their bishop, assisted by some of his clergy, and it is presumed that the work is going on. The four Gospels are in the press at Bombay and nearly completely printed...Some of the elders of the church were asked whether they were willing to distribute the Malayalim Scriptures, if they were aided in the expense. "We are most willing," they said...A Malayalim translation ought certainly to have been made before now; but we have had in later times neither educated individuals nor competent means. Our three colleges have been destroyed...

As to your proposal of circulating the Scriptures in the vernacular tongue, all the fathers of our church will unite with me in declaring that we will most cheerfully do it, if we have the funds to perform so good a work. One of the elders stepped forward and said, "To convince you of our earnest desire to have the Bible in the Malayalim tongue, I need only mention that I have lately translated the Gospel of St. Matthew for the benefit of my own children. It is often borrowed by the other families. It is not in fine language, but the people love to read it." It was then proposed to them that a standard translation of the Malayalim should be prepared and sent to each of the fifty-five churches, on condition that each church should multiply the copies and circulate them among the people. "We accept your offer," said the priests, "with thankfulness"...

The Roman Catholic bishop, the Vicar Apostolic of the Pope in India, has consented to the circulation of the Scriptures throughout his diocese, so that there are upwards of 200,000 persons who are ready to receive the Malayalim Bible.

DAY 87
On Christian India: Part 3 of 3
by Henry Martyn
(Excerpted from *Sermons*, published by Crocker and Brewster, Boston, Massachusetts in 1822)

Galatians 6:10

Four: we come now to the last class of native Christians, the Cingalese. On the Island of Ceylon, in the year 1801, the number of native schools amounted to one hundred and seventy; and the number of native Protestant Christians exceeded 342,000. The Christians professing the religion of the Church of Rome are supposed to be still more numerous. No part of India offers such encouragements to attempts at moral improvement as Ceylon. The New Testament has been translated into Cingalese, and printed at Columbo at the direction of the government for the purpose of supplying the natives professing Christianity. For this information the Bible Society, from whose last report we have obtained it, profess themselves indebted to Sir Alexander Johnstone, late Chief Justice on that island; and in consequence of his representation, they have determined to set aside as much as can be spared from the expenses necessary to execute their vast plans to promote the circulation of the Cingalese Scriptures.

***

It is now time for the converts to have their ministers and pastors come from themselves. But no one can ever become qualified for the ministry without studying the Bible. On the other hand, there is every reason to believe that if they had free access to the Scriptures soon some would be found competent to teach others. It has always been so in every country; they were first called and directed by the missionary, and after a little time went on by themselves. If the Indians have not yet done so, it is because of their unique circumstances. The former possessors of the country have been generally their enemies. Their degradation paralyzes them. If you make a great effort, and lift them but a little, you will soon find that they will "awake and put on their strength." They will shake themselves from the dust and arise—they will advance rapidly in knowledge and go on without your aid. Should we, however, be deceived in our hope of seeing them organized and regular pastors administering the holy ordinances, it is at all events impossible to believe that the people with the Scriptures in their possession would long remain in their present deplorable condition. They would read it in their houses; they would teach it to their children; they would talk of it in the way...

The persons for whom we plead also call our Lord theirs, and hold His word in the same reverence we do. They will not eye the sacred volume with suspicion, but seize it with delight, as a book they have often longed to see. The undertaking in which we urge you to engage has nothing in the nature of it to which anyone can reasonably object. The means of accomplishing the desired purpose are beyond dispute—the success is certain—for God Himself has declared concerning the word which goes out of His mouth that it shall not return void: "It shall accomplish that which I please, and it shall prosper wherever I sent it" [Isaiah 55:11]. The frame of heaven may pass away, much more so the schemes of men, but "My word," said Christ, "shall not pass away" [Matthew 24:35]...Let us reflect a moment upon the unhappy state of those who live without a Bible, but especially of those who die without one...The Bible, alas! Is a treasure, which they never had the happiness to possess...The Lord who loves our brethren, who gave His life for them and for you, who gave you the Bible before them, and now wills that they should receive it from you; He will reward you. They cannot repay you; but you shall be repaid at the resurrection of the just. The King Himself will say to you, "In as much as you have done it unto one of the least of these, My brethren, you have done it unto Me" [Matthew 25:40].

DAY 88
The Rejected Offering
by M. S. Hutton

(Excerpted from his sermon delivered to the Foreign Missionary Society
of New York and Brooklyn, published by Almon Merwin, Bible House, New York,
New York in 1853)

*"I have no pleasure in you, says the Lord of hosts,
and I will not accept an offering from your hand."*
Malachi 1:10

The greatest curse which God could inflict in this life upon His people would be to deny them the pleasure and privilege of advancing His cause and kingdom. It would prevent us from conferring upon all others any real blessing: it would exclude us from all connection with the plans and purposes of God, making us enemies of God and people; it would render this life comparatively worthless and aimless; it would place us on the same terrible and malevolent platform with Satan and the fallen angels; it would deprive us of much present joy and all heavenly rewards…

Yes, truly our glory would be taken away if God was to refuse our missionary offerings. Think for a single moment of the consequences which would follow at this moment if God was to say in His wrath to His Church, "I have no pleasure in you, neither will I accept an offering from your hand. Call home your missionaries, close your churches; I ask no song, I will hear no prayer, I will bless no exertions." Would it not be like forbidding the sun to rise and shine upon the labors of all? If God was to forbid us to labor for the support of our bodies, the human family would perish; and if He was to forbid the spiritual efforts of His Church, His Church would die, and all the hopes and blessings which she brings would perish with her, and our earth become what the Bible describes hell to be—a place where love, hope, joy, and peace have departed forever.

We learn from this subject that the minister of the gospel who does not give his people full and frequent opportunities to advance the cause of Christ is, in fact, his people's enemy, and robs both them and himself of a great blessing.

We learn that they who neglect to pray for the perishing heathen and the coming of Christ's kingdom, and who find fault with the variety of the calls made on their generosity where the soul's salvation is involved, are finding fault with their privileges, are preferring Barabbas to Christ, and refusing one of the greatest blessings which God can bestow.

We see that no Christian should be prevented from aiding in the advance of Christ's kingdom by the consideration that one can do only a little. However, that little is too great a privilege to be rejected, even though it may be but a cup of cold water. It has sometimes been asked when contributions are being made for the kingdom of Christ, "Shall this or that poor person who is, possibly, an object of charity, be requested to give of out of poverty?" I reply in the light of our theme: "What has that person done that they should be deprived of this privilege?" Why should we say to anyone, "God will not accept an offering at your hands?"

***

And lastly, if the Church of Christ does not treasure as she should the blessing of being allowed to make her offerings to the Lord, may not our offended God say to her now, as He did to Israel, "I have no pleasure in you, and I will not accept an offering from your hand"? Israel fell because of unbelief. Remember that we stand only by faith. It is possible—no, my brothers and sisters, if we look down on our mercies and neglect our privileges, it is certain—that God will reject us, as He did Israel of old if we refuse to preach the gospel to every creature. God will take from us the privilege and give it to others.

DAY 89
The Will for the Deed
by George Matheson
(Excerpted from *Searchings in the Silence*, published by Hodder and Stoughton, London, England in 1894)

Your feet shod with the preparation of the gospel of peace.
Ephesians 6:15

"Shod with the *preparation* of the gospel," "shod with *preparedness* to run on the message of peace." Is that all we should expect from the walk of Christian life? To *prepare* to run seems a small thing. Why does not Paul say that the feet of the soldier of Christ have been hardened by the actual running—strengthened, not by the *preparation*, but by the *proclamation* of the gospel? Because, if he had said that, he would have cut off the larger part of the army.

It is only a limited number of Christ's soldiers who are allowed to serve in the field; the largest part have to be content with *readiness* to serve. The souls who do great things in the world are the minority; the mass can only *will* to do them. I may say, "How beautiful on the mountains are the feet of him that brings good tidings" [Isaiah 52:7] and yet my own feet may be unmoved.

I may be forbidden to join the band of active workers. I may be an invalid. I may be weighed down with the care of an invalid. I may be struggling with poverty. I may be a victim of nerves. I may be encumbered with many household duties. I may be hopelessly ordinary. In all these things my Father says to me "Stay at home." But, in spite of all these things, I have the will to go; I would go if these did not prohibit me; I do go in spirit every day. I carry messages with the feet of my heart. I am armed with the preparation to be a Christian soldier—with the readiness to serve if service were possible. I have given to God my will to give, and He has accepted it as my uniform; He has ordered for me a soldier's pay.

Isaac, you son of Abraham, are you lamenting the lack of your father's armor? Are you sighing that while he conquered nations you are only permitted to dig wells? No, but the sigh is itself a display to you. Your feet are shod with the preparation, the readiness to go. Yours is the red fire of Mount Moriah, though it is all within you. Yours is the resistance to the point of shedding blood, though the fight is seen by none. Yours is the sacrifice unto death, although you did not die. In your wells of water God beholds the possibilities of the deep sea. In your petty difficulties God hears the roar of the great battle. In the troubles of your tiny pool God credits to you the wrestling of the angel.

Your territory is narrow but your heart is wide; stand up and take your crown—the crown of desires unfulfilled, the prize for mighty deeds designed to do. Your monument is side by side with Abraham's: his has the inscription, "the man who journeyed." yours has the tribute of a larger hope, "the one who was prepared to go."

DAY 90
Christianity As Final Religion: Part 1 of 5
by Samuel M. Zwemer
(Excerpted from *Christianity the Final Religion*, published by Eerdmans-Sevensma
Company, Grand Rapids, Michigan in 1920)

***

Christ came to destroy race-barriers and race-hatred. He gave
womanhood its place, childhood its rights, the slave his freedom,
and the barbarian welcome. In the fellowship of Jesus Christ, His
love, His mercy, and His Kingdom there is neither Jew nor Greek,
male nor female, slave nor free, Roman nor barbarian. Wherever the
followers of Jesus Christ have disobeyed this law of His Kingdom—
through race-hatred and prejudice—they have misrepresented that
Kingdom which has no borders, and in which the humble alone
receive citizenship.

The non-Christian religions without exception condemn women by
the principles of their teaching to the place of property or slave.
Buddhism proclaims that no woman as woman can be saved. What
a contrast this is with the teaching of Jesus Christ to the outcast
Samaritan woman at the well. Islam has degraded womanhood by
the lives and the literature of its apostles, from the days of
Mohammed and Ali until our own day.

Christ, the founder of Christianity, is not the son of any nation or
people, but the Son of Man, the Perfect Man. Mohammed was an
Arab; that is his boast, and the result has been that as long as his
religion abides, it is tied hand and foot to a civilization based upon
the Arabian institutions of the seventh century. To be a true Muslim
one must copy the pattern once for all laid down, and it is an
arabesque [ornamental design]—without life.

"So while the world rolls on from age to age

And realms of thought expand,
The letter stands without expanse or range,
Stiff as a dead man's hand."

Confucius was a Chinese scholar, Buddha an Indian ascetic, Socrates a Greek philosopher. The systems of thought and philosophy to which they gave birth are therefore indelibly national. But Jesus of Nazareth, although a Jew by lineage, was not a Jew in his limitations or ideals or teachings. He was neither an Occidental [Westerner] nor an Oriental in the popular meaning of these words. He combined in Himself all the ideals of East and West, without any of their limitations. In Him we see the Alpha and Omega of ideal humanity. This thought is beautifully expressed by an Indian writer, M. C. Roy, who for more than twenty years has been headmaster of a mission school at Lucknow. The following lines were written in reply to [Rudyard] Kipling:

"Oh, East is East, and West is West, the twain
Shall never meet!—so sings the sage his song.
One clear crescendo, as though nothing wrong.
And naught but truth was uttered in that strain!

"Now, ye who rush to swell the score of such
Half-truths and hybrid thoughts, come listen ye.
To one that, all unlearning, learnt to be
Responsive to the Spirit's guiding touch:
Love that loves all, and dies to love again—
The love that spans all gulfs and scales all heights,
That breaks all bars and holds in high disdain
All that parts man from man, and disunites—
This God-Man's Love that breathes sweet peace and rest,
Can blend, and blend in one, both East and West."

DAY 91
Christianity As Final Religion: Part 2 of 5
by Samuel M. Zwemer
(Excerpted from *Christianity the Final Religion*, published by Eerdmans-Sevensma Company, Grand Rapids, Michigan in 1920)

Christ's purpose and command and promise in regard to His mission are worldwide. This is a unique characteristic even of Old Testament prophecy, that it sweeps the whole horizon and includes in its plan the final enlightenment, the salvation of all nations. The sixty-seventh Psalm, and the sixtieth chapter of Isaiah are examples. In no other book of all the sacred books of the East do we find such expressions regarding the universality of God's love, and His all-embracing purpose. The Great Commission in its four-part form finds no parallel even in Islam or Buddhism, although both are missionary faiths. One ceases to be a Hindu by crossing the ocean. Islam has for the most part been self-limited to the heat belt, on account of its prayer ritual; but Christianity has gone to every nation and climate on its triumphal march. Of no other religious leader have people dared to write that "every knee shall bow and every tongue confess"—only as regards Jesus Christ. The guiding principle of the missionary enterprise—the evangelization of the world in this generation—is inconceivable when applied to any other religion; and it never has been conceived by any other enthusiast or disciple of other religions.

The laws and ritual of the Christian religion are so simple and universal that they are possible everywhere and for everybody. The New Testament knows of no sacred place or shrine, river or mountain. When the Samaritan woman referred to the sacred character of Mount Gerizim, Jesus answered: "Neither in this mountain nor in Jerusalem shall you worship the Father...God is a Spirit and they who worship Him must worship Him in spirit and truth" [John 4:23-24]. Whenever Christian tradition or practice has laid claim to special holiness for any particular place, it was in direct conflict with the teaching of Christ and the world mission of His apostles. According to Islam, prayer is impossible at all times or in all places or by everybody. A prayer at Mecca has more value, mathematically and spiritually, than at Medina; a prayer at Medina has more value than one at Jerusalem. In Hinduism the three sacred rivers are the Indus, then the Sarasvati, and then the Ganges. There are hundreds of *tirthas*—sacred places for merit and pilgrimage. The whole prayer ritual in Buddhism and Islam is artificial and practically impossible for women and children.

In Muslim works of theology there are whole sections on the occasions, method, variety and effect of purification; on the different kinds of water allowed; on the times when prayer is not permitted, and on the details of posture and bowing, which would be foolish were they not heartbreaking. How simple are the teachings of Christ! How universal the injunctions of His apostles— "Pray without ceasing"—"I will that people pray everywhere." Christianity commands no public or private duty which cannot be performed because of age, sex, region or climate. In this respect its very sacraments are simple and appropriate, and its form of worship can be observed in catacombs [tombs] or cathedrals, huts or palaces, in prisons or in the trenches, by land or by sea, at the poles and at the tropics. Jesus Christ is the only religious leader who ever identified His mission and His message with childhood. We cannot conceive of Confucius or Buddha or Mohammed saying: "Allow the little children to come to Me...of such is the kingdom of heaven" [Mark 10:14].

DAY 92
Christianity As Final Religion: Part 3 of 5
by Samuel M. Zwemer

(Excerpted from *Christianity the Final Religion*, published by Eerdmans-Sevensma
Company, Grand Rapids, Michigan in 1920)

The gospel, that is the good news of the person and work and
power of Jesus Christ, has been translated into all languages, and
what is far more remarkable, is translatable into every human
speech. Most of the sacred books of the other religions are difficult
to translate and in many cases impossible for translation because of
their style and contents. The former is often artificial and highly
poetic, or in such literary form as to defy translation; but the Bible
has proved as eloquent as it is comprehensible in all languages. Its
style is human and its form universal. Many of the Hindu books,
e.g., the *Dharam Sindhu*, which describes the holy festival and the
"Tantras" that deal with Sakti worship, are obscene and horrible
beyond belief. Who would care to give a popular, literal translation
of the thirty-third or sixty-sixth chapter of the Qu'ran?

Although other sacred books have been translated into languages
not their own, they are the exception and not the rule. Most of these
translations were the result of Christian scholarship, and were not
spontaneous. The Bible, however, has won its readers and proved its
popularity from the earliest centuries. In days when each copy had
to be made by hand, the scribes multiplied only such books as were
in demand; yet we are told that "the plays of Aeschylus survive in
about fifty manuscripts, while of the New Testament we possess
over 4,000 Greek manuscripts, more or less complete, besides 8,000
Latin manuscripts, of the Vulgate version." The earliest book to be
printed in Europe was the Latin Bible, and one hundred editions of
it had appeared during the first half-century of printing. The most
popular modern English author is Charles Dickens, and it has been
computed that since *Pickwick* appeared, 25,000,000 copies of his

books have gone out into the world. But during the last four years of war [WWI] alone, the Bible societies have circulated forty million portions of the Scriptures in four hundred and thirty-seven languages. The Bible is the best-selling book in the world.

Christ has begun to occupy the dominant place in the world of law and culture and morals. When Pilate wrote above the Cross, "Jesus of Nazareth King," he unwittingly foretold that Christ should have dominion in the Latin world of law—civil and international; in the Greek world of literature and culture; and in the Hebrew world of ethics and religion. The flags of at least two of the world's greatest empires bear the sign of the Cross. The same symbol was fittingly chosen for the international ministry of aid and friendship to all who suffer the horrors of war—the Red Cross. The principles of international law are based on the teaching of the Sermon on the Mount. The violations of international law, the cruel wrongs of exploitations, or the bad administration of subject colonies are condemned by the conscience of humanity because that conscience has to some degree been Christianized. Christians have often failed, and Christian nations, but not Christianity and Christ. "The war," said an Egyptian paper in 1915, "has proved not the failure of Christ or Christianity, but of Christians." The old Greek civilization, its music, sculpture, painting, architecture and literature, have been literally led captive in the train of Jesus Christ. All the fine arts have become finer because of His coming into the world and His death on the Cross. All the world has gone after Him for new ideals. Whether this was done with reverence and awe, or whether art stripped Jesus, as the soldiers did of His clothing and, having rejected Him, gambled over his seamless robe, does not detract from our argument. The history of music, sculpture, painting and architecture cannot leave out the story of the gospel and must give some answer to explain the preeminence of Jesus.

DAY 93
Christianity As Final Religion: Part 4 of 5
by Samuel M. Zwemer
(Excerpted from *Christianity the Final Religion*, published by Eerdmans-Sevensma
Company, Grand Rapids, Michigan in 1920)

The ethics of the New Testament have become the international standard of right and wrong, the yardstick by which people measure conduct. In no other way can we explain the fact that Hindus are today reading Christianity into Hinduism, and Muslims are rejoicing when they discover traditions (however obscure) which point to the Christ-like character of their prophet. Christianity has in recent years exercised an immense influence upon Japanese life and thought, quite apart from its acknowledged doctrinal effect upon Buddhism and Shintoism in the past. The Babi-Behai faith, which claims to be the universal religion, has borrowed not only its ethical standards and doctrinal terminology, but its very claim to be universal, from Christianity. All of the Islamic sects which denounce polygamy [multiple marriages], concubines [mistresses], divorce and slavery as contrary to Islam, damage the facts of history in order to raise the Arabian to the level of the Nazarene. In the Qu'ran and in orthodox Muslim tradition, Christ is the only sinless prophet, untouched by Satan at birth, victorious over all temptation, and who returns at last from heaven to establish righteousness.

Christ's idea of God, indeed, His revelation of God, is the highest and most comprehensive conception of deity that the human mind has ever expressed or imagined. A God who is at once transcendent in His unapproachable majesty, God the Father of all, above all, full of glory, whom no person can see; inherent in creation and through His Spirit in human hearts; incarnate in "the Son of His love in whom we have redemption through His blood" [Ephesians 1:7]. "The God whom people know outside of Jesus Christ," says Alexander Maclaren, "is a poor, nebulous thing; an idea and not a reality." No one would ever think of consulting Confucius, the sage of China, on the subject of God. On other matters his teaching is often very illuminating and helpful, but on this subject he taught practically nothing. "Where in all China," writes Charles L. Ogilvie of Peking, "can one find anything that equates with what the ten-year-old Christian child knows about God, the Father of our Lord Jesus Christ? Would anyone who knows this God be attracted by the hundred and one imaginary Buddhas, the innumerable Pu'sas, with the merciful Kwam Kin at the head, the Gemmy Emperor, who rules on Tai-shan; Kwan Ti, the god of war, or Allah, whose compassion is imprisoned by fate? He who was called the 'brightness of the Father's glory and the express image of His person' [Hebrews 1:3] has so flooded the world with light that no one who has seen the face of the heavenly Father is at all drawn to the gods of the nations."

Islam has risen higher than any of the other non-Christian faiths in its conception of God, and yet in four particulars has as conspicuously failed to reach the New Testament or even the Old Testament idea: (a) There is no Fatherhood; (b) There is an absence of all emphasis on the supreme attribute of love with all its great implications; (c) Allah is not absolutely, unchangeably and eternally just. It is possible, as some allege, that the western Church may have over-emphasized the forensic aspect [related to law] of God's holiness and righteousness. But the Bible and the human conscience in all ages also emphasize this truth. It is found in Greek theism [belief in many gods]. The Judge of all the earth must do right. Allah, however, makes it easy for men; neither in his holiness nor in his mercy is his righteousness manifested; and (d) Add to this that there is, as Raymond Lull pointed out, a lack of balance in Allah's attributes. Without an atonement, how could there be real balance? Christ is the final revelation of God as regards His being and His attributes. "He who has seen Me," He said, "has seen the Father" [John 14:9]. "No one has seen God at any time, the only begotten Son has declared Him."

DAY 94
Christianity As Final Religion: Part 5 of 5
by Samuel M. Zwemer
(Excerpted from *Christianity the Final Religion*, published by Eerdmans-Sevensma
Company, Grand Rapids, Michigan in 1920)

Christ combines in Himself the highest ideal of character and of redemption. All religions have ideals of character and ways of salvation. They all start from the same point in response to the hunger of the human heart for rest and forgiveness, and in the search for higher life. But they all fail to reach the goal.

"Not all the blood of beasts slain on [their] altars can give the guilty conscience peace or wash away the stain." Aside from every theory of the atonement, the fact remains that Christ satisfies the human heart as a sufficient Savior. Tens of thousands of every nation and tribe and kindred testify:

> "Thou, O Christ, art all I want,
> More than all in Thee I find."

Only of this Man was it said, "Behold the Lamb of God that takes away the sin of the world" [John 1:29]. The character of Jesus is incomparable. He is the holiest among the mighty and the mightiest among the holy. "By the confession of friend and foe alike," says Bosworth Smith, the apologist [defender] for Mohammed, "the character of Jesus of Nazareth stands alone in its spotless purity and its unapproachable majesty." The non-Christian religions one and all present no perfect moral ideal. Not one of the founders of ethnic religions ever used words like Christ did: "Which of you proves Me of sin?" None of them claimed to be morally the ideal and goal of humanity. Jesus said He was "the Way, the Truth and the Life," and He proved it.

He proves it today. He offers the strongest possible evidence for the truth of His teaching, namely, experience. Christianity is not primarily a religion based on human or divine authority, although it has the authority of Divine revelation through human channels and of Him who claimed to be the Son of God. Nor does Christianity base its claims on tradition—though unbroken tradition—as does Islam or later Judaism. Nor does Christ, although He worked miracles, appeal to power as an argument for the truth of His teaching. Christianity was not propagated by force or by the sword. Those that seized it were ignorant of or blind to the spirit of their Master. Nor did Christ depend on the logic of argument to convince men, although He spoke as no man ever spoke. He appealed to the freedom of the human will by inviting people to try the experiment of His friendship and fellowship: "Follow Me," "Come to Me," "Ask and you shall receive," "If anyone will do His will he shall know," "You will not come to Me," "Will you also go away," and "the one that comes to Me I will in no wise cast out."

The experiment to which Christ here challenges the human heart has been tried for twenty centuries by hundreds of millions and never yet failed. Those who draw near to Christ enter His friendship, look up into His face and clasp His pierced hand, and always experience two things: First, a sense of spiritual and moral bankruptcy, and then a sense of spiritual and moral asset and affluence. The character and the demands of Jesus produce the first; His cross and resurrection the second. Paul the self-righteous becomes the "chief of sinners"...Those who have had this experience have no further doubt that Christ is the only Savior, and Christianity the final religion. For them the two eternities, past and future, and the whole period lying in between are united and controlled by one purpose—redemption through Christ. He is the Alpha and the Omega. In all things He has first place. He will yet reconcile all things to Himself, whether things upon the earth or things in the heavens. He will restore the lost harmony of the universe, because to Him every knee shall bow and every tongue confess...

DAY 95
The Field is the World: Part 1 of 3
by Francis Wayland
(from his sermon, "The Moral Dignity of the Missionary Enterprise,"
delivered to The Boston Baptist Foreign Mission Society on October 26, 1823;
and to The Salem Bible Translation Society on November 4, 1823, published by
James Loring, Boston, Massachusetts in 1824)

"The field is the world…"
Matthew 13:38

The objective of the missionary enterprise embraces every child of Adam. It is as vast as the race to whom its operations are necessarily limited. It would confer upon every individual on earth all that intellectual or moral cultivation can bestow. It would rescue a world from the indignation and wrath, tribulation and anguish reserved for every person that does evil, and give it a title to glory, honor, and immortality. You see, then, that our object is not only to affect every individual of the species, but to affect them in the momentous extremes of infinite happiness and infinite woe. And now we ask: What purpose ever undertaken by anyone can compare with this same design of evangelizing the world? Patriotism itself fades away before it, and acknowledges the supremacy of an enterprise which seizes, with so strong a grasp, upon both the temporal and eternal destinies of all humanity…

The missionary undertaking is arduous enough to call into action the noblest energies of everyone.
Its difficulty is explained in one term, our *Field is the World*. Our object is to achieve an entire moral revolution in the whole human race. Its difficulty then results because of its magnitude. I need not say to an audience acquainted with the nature of the human mind that a large moral mass is not easily and permanently affected. A little leaven does not soon leaven the whole lump. To produce a

change even of speculative opinion upon a single nation is an undertaking not easily accomplished. In the case before us, not a nation but a world is to be saved; therefore the change which we would achieve is far from being merely speculative. If any person is in Christ, they are a new creature. Nothing short of this new creation will fulfill our purpose. We go out not to persuade others to turn from one idol to another, but to turn universally from idols to serve the living God. We call upon those who are earthly, sensual, devilish, to set their affections on things above. We go out urging everyone to forsake every cherished lust, and present themselves a living sacrifice, holy and acceptable unto God. And this mighty moral revolution is to be achieved not in a family, a tribe, or a nation, but in a world which lies in wickedness.

We have to operate upon a race divided into different nations, speaking a thousand different languages, under every different form of government, from absolute apathy to unbridled tyranny, and inhabiting every district of a country—wholesome or deadly—from the equator to the poles. To all these nations must the gospel be sent, into all these languages must the Bible be translated, to all these climates—healthy or deadly—must the missionary penetrate, and under all these forms of government, mild or despotic, must a person preach Christ and Him crucified.

Frequently, we shall interfere with the more shameful interests of people; and we expect them to increase the difficulties of our undertaking. If we can turn the heathen to God, many sources of unholy traffic will be dried up, and many conveniences of unholy gratification will be taken away. Consequently, we may expect that the traffickers in human flesh, the disciples of greed, and the devotees of pleasure will be against us. From the heathen themselves we have the blackest darkness of ignorance to dispel. We have to assault systems distinguished for their antiquity, and interwoven with everything that is proud in a nation's history. Above all, we have to oppose the depravity of the human heart, grown still more ingrained by ages of continuing unrestrained evil...

The Field is the World: Part 2 of 3
by Francis Wayland
(from his sermon, "The Moral Dignity of the Missionary Enterprise,"
delivered to The Boston Baptist Foreign Mission Society on October 26, 1823;
and to The Salem Bible Translation Society on November 4, 1823, published by
James Loring, Boston, Massachusetts in 1824)

"The field is the world..."
Matthew 13:38

This enterprise requires superior wisdom in the missionary who goes abroad, as well as in those who manage the concerns of a missionary society at home. Those who go out unprotected to preach Christ to despotic or badly-governed nations must be wise as serpents and harmless as a doves. They must combine undeviating firmness upon everything essential with the most sacrificial capacity for all that is unimportant. And thus while they go out in the spirit and power of Elijah, they must at the same time become all things to all people that by all means they may gain some. Great abilities are also required in those who conduct the mission at home. They must awaken, energize, and direct the sentiments of a very large portion of the community in which they reside, while at the same time, through a hundred different agents, they exert a powerful influence upon half as many nations a thousand or ten thousand miles off...

The missionary undertaking calls for perseverance—a perseverance of that character, which, having once formed its purpose, never wavers from it until death. And if ever this attribute has been so exhibited as to challenge the respect of every person of feeling, it has been in such instances as are recorded in the history of the missions to Greenland and to the South Sea Islands, where we beheld missionaries, for fifteen or twenty years, suffer everything but martyrdom, and then, seeing no fruit from their labor, resolve to labor on until death, if so they might at last save one unenlightened heathen from the error of their ways.

This undertaking calls for self-denial of the highest and holiest character. Those who engage in it must, at the very outset, dismiss every wish to demand for anything but the mere favor of God. Their first act is a voluntary exile from all that a refined education loves; and every other act must be in unison with this. The salvation of the heathen is the object for which they sacrifice—and are willing to sacrifice—everything that the heart clings to on earth. For this objective they would live; for this they would die; no, they would live anywhere, and die anyhow, if it be they might rescue one soul from everlasting woe.

***

But above all, the missionary undertaking requires faith, in its holiest and most supreme exercise. And let it not be supposed that we speak at random when we mention the exaltation of faith. "Whatever," says the British moralist, "withdraws us from the power of the senses, whatever makes the past, the distant, or the future predominate over the present, advances us in the dignity of thinking beings." And when we speak of faith, we refer to a principle which gives substance to things hoped for and evidence to things not seen; which, bending her keen glance on the eternal weight of glory, makes it a constant motive to holy enterprise; which, fixing her eagle eye upon the infinite of future, makes it bear well upon the purposes of today; a principle which enables a poor feeble tenant of the dust to take strong hold upon the perfections of Jehovah; and, fastening one's hopes to the very throne of the Eternal, "bid earth roll, nor feel its idle whirl." This principle is the unfailing support of the missionaries through the long years of tedious journey; and, when they are compared with the heroes of this world, it is unique to them. As much, then, as the Christian enterprise calls into being this one principle, the noblest that can attach to the character of a creature, by so much does its execution surpass in magnificence every other enterprise.

DAY 97
The Field is the World: Part 3 of 3
by Francis Wayland
(from his sermon, "The Moral Dignity of the Missionary Enterprise,"
delivered to The Boston Baptist Foreign Mission Society on October 26, 1823;
and to The Salem Bible Translation Society on November 4, 1823, published by
James Loring, Boston, Massachusetts in 1824)

"The field is the world…"
Matthew 13:38

Let us consider the means by which this moral revolution is to be achieved.
It is, in a word, by the preaching of Jesus Christ and Him crucified. It is by going out and telling the lost children of humankind that God so loved the world that He gave His only begotten Son to die for them, and by all the eloquence of such an appeal to urge them for Christ's sake to be reconciled unto God. This is the lever by which, we believe, the moral universe is to be raised; this is the instrument by which a sinful world is to be saved.

***

We see that all which is really horrible in the misery of humankind results from the disease of their moral nature. If this can be healed, people may be restored to happiness. Now the gospel of Jesus Christ is the remedy devised by Omniscience [all-knowing God] specifically for this purpose, and therefore we do certainly know that it will inevitably succeed.

It is easy to see that the universal obedience to the command, You shall love the Lord your God with all your heart, and your neighbor as yourself, would make this world a heaven. But nothing other than the gospel of Christ can persuade others to this obedience. Reason cannot do it; philosophy cannot do it; civilization cannot do it. The cross of Christ alone has power to bend the stubborn will to obedience and melt the frozen heart to love. For, said one who had experienced its effectiveness, the love of Christ compels us, because we thus judge that if one died for all, then all were dead; and that He died for all, that they which live should not live for themselves, but for Him who died for them and rose again.

And lastly, we know from the word of the living God that it will be successful until this whole world has been redeemed from the effects of man's first disobedience. As truly as I live, says Jehovah, all the earth shall be filled with the glory of the Lord. Ask of Me, He says to His Son, and I will give You the heathen for Your inheritance, and the uttermost parts of the earth for Your possession. In the Revelation which He gave to His servant John of things which should shortly come to pass: I heard, said the apostle, great voices in heaven, saying, The kingdoms of this world are become the kingdoms of our Lord, and of His Christ, and He shall reign forever and ever. Here then is the ground of our unwavering confidence. Heaven and earth shall pass away, but not one jot or one tittle [the tiniest thing] shall pass from the word of God until all is fulfilled. Such, then, are the means on which we rely for the accomplishment of our objective, and such are the grounds upon which we rest our confidence for success. And now deliberately consider the nature of the missionary enterprise. Reflect upon the dignity of its purpose; the high moral and intellectual powers which are to be called out in its execution; the simplicity, compassion, and effectiveness of the means by which all this is to be achieved; and we ask you, Does not every other enterprise to which one ever put out his or her strength dwindle into insignificance before that of preaching Christ crucified to a lost and perishing world?

***

May God by His grace enable us so to act, that on that day we may meet with joy the record of the doings of this day; and to His name shall be the glory in Christ. Amen.

DAY 98
The Song of the Lord
by Amy Carmichael
(Excerpted from *Overweights of Joy*, published by Fleming H. Revell Company,
New York, New York in 1906)

Sometimes it may seem to us that our prayer life would develop
more easily under easier conditions...But God's flowers grow best
in places where only an angel would have thought of planting
them...Perhaps if we could shut our eyes on the world's way of
looking at things, and go to sleep with our head on a stone, we
should see all the obstructions, all the impossible, changed to a
ladder beside us, set on the earth, the top reaching heaven...The
battle is not imitation war. The evolution, intrigue, impact are most
tremendous realities. And yet, looking not at some little hand-picked
regiment, but widely over the army of God, does it not appear that a
spirit foreign to the soldier has now infected us, and so dealt with us
that what the first soldier-missionary meant by conflict, whether in
service or prayer, is something we hardly understand, and the battle
cries of God's elder warriors sound harshly in our ears? Is there not
something lacking in nerve, and tendon, and muscle, and bone? Do
we not see some things through a mist and a glamour, knowing not,
yes, refusing to know it—for that spirit has dulled our soul's vision
and obscured it—that it is but a mist and a glamour?...

"Braver souls for truth may bleed;
Ask us not of noble deed!
Small our share in Christ's redemption—
From His war we claim exemption.
Not for us the cup was drained;
Not for us the crown of thorn
On His bleeding brow was borne:
Not for us the spear was stained
With the blood from out His side;

Not for us the Crucified
Let His hands and feet be torn!
On the list we come but low:
Not for us the cross was taken,
Us no bugle call can waken
To the combat, soldier fashion."

We would not say it. We consider it bad taste. But do we never live it? Consider: let us view ourselves in the light of that most awful sacrifice. Do we believe in Calvary? What difference does it make that we believe? How does this belief affect the spending of our one possession—life? Are we playing it away? Does it strike us as fanatical to do anything more serious? Are we too refined to be in earnest? Too polite to be strenuous? Too cool to burn? God, open our eyes, and touch our hearts, and break us down with the thought of the Love that redeemed us, and a sight of souls as He sees them, and of ourselves as we are, and not as people suppose we are, lest we sail in some pleasure boat of our own creation over the gliding waters that glide to the river of death.

***

We have seldom touched on the deeper misery we know of and see signs of, because there are some notes which cannot bear to be struck twice: and because not pity, but obedience, is the inhibiting force. We would not draw one to come by the insignificant thread of pity, or by the other, still more slender, sentimental love. The refrain of some sweet hymn, the touching description of sorrowful eyes, and a wistfulness inexpressible—these things have voices which call, but the power that holds is not in them. Those of us who have come to Muslim or heathen lands for life, if God wills, know that what keeps us here is something stronger than sympathy. And yet, though we would not deliver our strongest call through it, misery, which no imagination can interpret too bitterly, looks at us everywhere, and through everything, with its mute appeal. There is ultimately only one sure way to end it. Are we showing the people this one sure way?

DAY 99
Harmony with God's Purpose: Part 1 of 2
by Arthur T. Pierson
(Excerpted from *The New Acts of the Apostles*, published by The Baker & Taylor Company, New York in 1894)

To work with God and on God's plan is the only real bliss, and the only sure success. Everything else is disappointment and failure. President Lincoln was once taunted by an adversary with the temporary defeat of political measures which he had adopted in the interests of the eternal principles of right. His noble reply was: "Defeat! If it were not one, but one hundred defeats, I should still pursue the same unchanging course." And, on another occasion, when, during the war for the Union, a timid man ventured to say: "I hope God will be on our side," Lincoln's response was: "My only anxiety is to be on God's side." And it was this man of an incarnate conscience whose heroic words were: "Let us believe that right makes might, and in that faith let us to the end dare to do our duty as we understand it." It is the same sentiment that [Frederick William] Faber crystallized into verse:

> "He always wins who sides with God;
> With him no chance is lost."

It is, therefore, of immense importance to us to know what God's plan is and then to take our place in it. As to the purpose of God in this dispensation, Anthony Grant has, in his Bampton Lectures, given a clear and brief statement: "That the gospel shall be preached in some places at all times, and in all places at some time." And beyond this we know very little. How large or rapid are to be the visible results in any one field is a matter never yet unveiled; it is one of the secret things that belong to the Lord our God. But what is revealed is His will that we should go into all the world and preach the gospel to every creature.

Then if, as George Bowen told Dr. Norman McLeod of himself, thirty years are spent in India without one known convert, we can still do our duty—for in God's eyes that is success; anything else, failure. The holiest aspiration in this doing of God's will on God's plan finds satisfaction. A divine ambition completely occupies the soul. This is the avenue to the purest, widest influence.

One may, at God's bidding, go into comparative seclusion and obscurity—as Bishop Butler, author of the famous "Analogy," into the little country parish of Stanhope, so that Archbishop Blackburne told Queen Caroline that he was "not dead, but buried"—but if it be at God's bidding it is no burial alive, except as a seed concealed for a crop. Butler, during that apparent burial, was writing that great work which revolutionized the thinking of that deistic age!

In great crises of Church history some word of God has become the rallying cry of His true followers. The motto of the Apostolic age was: "Christ died for our sins, and rose again, according to the Scriptures." During the Lutheran Reformation, the watchword was: "The just shall live by faith." And, for this age of missions, what is a more fitting battle-cry than that which has been spontaneously chosen by the Student Volunteers in their "New Crusade":

The evangelization of the world in this generation!

This now famous motto has been traced to me when I first expressed it at the inauguration of this movement at Mount Hermon, Massachusetts, eight years ago. But the fact is, I got this motto from Acts 13:22 and 36, where the Holy Spirit says of David that God in him found a man after His own heart, who would fulfill all His will, and that he served his own generation by the will of God. Let us write that divine motto on all our banners!

How much is included here! *Sovereignty*—a divine Master; *Service*—a world's evangelization; *Sphere*—our own generation; a *Secret* and *Signal*—the will of God.

Harmony with God's Purpose: Part 2 of 2
by Arthur T. Pierson
(Excerpted from *The New Acts of the Apostles*, published by The Baker & Taylor
Company, New York in 1894)

A most expressive word is here [Acts 13:36] translated as "served"—it means to be an under-rower, and refers to the ancient galleys with their banks of oars, where every man who held an oar served under the control of the pilot. All God asks of us is to take the place which He assigns, and there do our work, watching His signal. When there is obedience to His will, there is sure to be cooperation with all other obedient souls, since they heed the same signal. The conception is magnificent. What a symphony of action! What a harmony of movement!—the oars rising and falling, dipping and dripping together, though the oarsmen do not see each other, and do not plan such cooperation; because one will sways all alike and controls the synchronisms and coincidences of history by a unity of universal plan.

And what identity with God! His will is His personality. To serve under that will as the all-controlling signal is to be one with Him— to be about our Father's business. What authority! For all is done in the name of the one Master. What holy audacity! As when David approached Goliath: "I come to you in the name of Jehovah, God of the armies of Israel, whom you have defied!" What security to one who does the will of God! "All things work together for good," in the orbit of obedience, which is a part of a universal system where God is Sun and Center! And what success! The very river of God is turned into the channel of our weak and wayward will—the mighty surge of His omnipotence, to turn the wheels of our life and action, and insure uninterrupted power and ultimate accomplishment.

And what is the natural sphere of every disciple's work and witness, if it is not one's own generation? No one can affect the past generations, and the best way to serve the future is by faithfulness to the present. One may in a sense belong to the whole race of humanity, but all are especially related to the human family as living on earth at the same period with one's self. Their claims on each individual are paramount, pressing, immediate, and imperative.

If the Church would come into harmony with God's purpose, here is the secret: He must be acknowledged as absolute Master, and His command must be the sole, sufficient authority. Service must be thought as part of a full discipleship and even a mature salvation; and that service must be accepted as proclaiming the gospel to every human creature. The will of God must be the one all-commanding signal which we watch, study, and obey. And our own generation must be, to our constant thought and prayer, the great and present sphere for our energetic and consecrated activity.

God has given a banner to those that fear Him, that it may be displayed because of the truth. And let the Church lift that banner high and bear it in the very front of the ranks and into the thick of the fight—with this motto emblazoned on it:

Serving our own generation by the will of God

100 Days with Christian Mystics

MISSIONS
Uniting with God's Heart for His Lost World

Final Thoughts

What is a Disciple?
by Bryan L. Herde

"Cannot...cannot...cannot..."
Luke 14:26, 27, 33

Give me an undivided heart...
Psalm 86:11

An undivided heart is essential for a disciple of Jesus Christ. It is a life given wholly and completely to the Lord for Him to do with as He pleases. This is in keeping with what Jesus said about Himself, "I seek not to please Myself but Him who sent Me" (John 5:30).

With all that has been said in this book about missions, missionaries, saving the lost, serving the Lord, going to the mission field, and more, it is critical that we do not miss the fact that He defined the purpose as "Go" in order "to make disciples." But before anyone can *make* disciples, one must *be* a disciple. That is why it is essential that we understand how the Lord defined who *is* and who *is not* a disciple.

First of all, a person must born again. This is the very heart of the Gospel of John, chapter 3. "In reply, Jesus declared, 'I tell you the truth, no one can see the kingdom of God unless they are born again...You should not be surprised at My saying, 'You *must* be born again.'" (emphasis added) This clearly-stated *must* is required before anything else can happen.

In that context, I pray and assume that you, the reader, have indeed been born again. This means that Christ is resident in your heart and that you are absolutely sealed by the Holy Spirit. That being said, we then move on to define what a disciple is. Luke 14:25-35 is the passage which most clearly declares how Jesus defines a disciple of His. I will quote just three of the verses:

> If anyone comes to Me and does not hate father and mother, wife and children, brothers and sisters—yes, even their own life—such a person *cannot* be My disciple. And whoever does not carry their cross and follow Me *cannot* be My disciple…In the same way, those of you who do not give up everything you have *cannot* be My disciples [emphasis added].

As you can see, a disciple is one who possesses nothing. All is given to Him. Please understand that in most cases, this does not mean that you are to sell everything you have and move to a monastery. Far from it. This refers to ownership, possession, loyalty, love and priorities of the heart. This is why I quoted Psalm 86:11 at the top. An undivided heart is what a disciple both agrees to and desires to have with and from God.

Singleness of heart (Psalm 86:11), singleness of focus (Matthew 6:22-23), singleness of purpose (Matthew 6:33) and singleness of life (Galatians 2:20) are the results of obedience to the requirements of Luke 14:25-35. A decision of one's will to surrender all and to depend upon God for all is a baseline definition of a disciple.

Men and women who have been born again and have fully given all they are and all they possess to the Lord are disciples of Jesus Christ.

Disciples are individuals who are controlled by the Holy Spirit (Romans 8). This does not mean that a disciple no longer sins. We are sinners saved by grace (Ephesians 2:8-9), but we still are sinners (1 John 1:9; 2:1-2). The issue is not that we sin or never sin, but who controls all.

Growing into spiritual maturity means that a disciple is advancing in intimacy with the Lord (Philippians 3:10), is dying to the world (Galatians 6:14), and abiding in Christ in order to bear much fruit (John 15:5).

In my opinion, the best definition of spiritual maturity, the evidence of a maturing life of a disciple, is found in Philippians 3:7-15:

> But whatever were gains to me I now consider loss for the sake of Christ. What is more, I consider everything a loss because of the surpassing worth of knowing Christ Jesus my Lord, for whose sake I have lost all things. I consider them garbage, that I may gain Christ and be found in Him, not having a righteousness of my own that comes from the law, but that which is through faith in Christ—the righteousness that comes from God on the basis of faith. I want to know Christ—yes, to know the power of His resurrection and participation in His sufferings, becoming like Him in His death, and so, somehow, attaining to the resurrection from the dead.
>
> Not that I have already obtained all this, or have already arrived at my goal, but I press on to take hold of that for which Christ Jesus took hold of me. Brothers and sisters, I do not consider myself yet to have taken hold of it. But one thing I do: Forgetting what is behind and straining toward what is ahead, I press on toward the goal to win the prize for which God has called me heavenward in Christ Jesus. All of us, then, **who are mature** should take such a view of things. And if on some point you think differently, that too God will make clear to you [emphasis added].

Being born again, becoming a disciple—as He defines it—and then being completely God's for Him to use as He pleases, that is being a true, mature disciple of Jesus Christ.

Making disciples is His command, and being a disciple is obedience to that command. A disciple will make other disciples, of that you can be sure. However, not many of us have the privilege of helping others to be born again, then helping those same individuals to grow up into mature, reproducing disciples. But in the Lord's hand, we will do our part for His glory and for the results He intends. Even the Apostle Paul recognized the partial role he played in the lives of others: "I planted the seed, Apollos watered it, but God made it grow" (1 Corinthians 3:6).

In this context, let's read the following passage written by Eli Smith:

> Whoever has given themselves wholly to the Savior's work, making it the great object of their life, whatever their specific employments may be, have found in it supreme delight. It is the bursting out of the generous emotions of a heart that swells with gratitude to Him to whom it is all is due. Have you, brothers and sisters, any of those generous emotions? Please enjoy the pleasure of expressing them in your lives. Be they expressed by giving in sacrifice to God what has heretofore been devoted to self, the very act will be a pleasurable enlargement of the soul. Self is too small an object for the vast active powers with which our Maker has given us. They can be fully expended upon nothing less than the great work He has made us for and assigned us.

> Give yourselves wholly to this work, though it is by still laboring upon your farm or at your place of business, and then will you find that for the first time you are in your proper place. You are doing just what God intended you should do, and the soul is satisfied. All is right. Do this and other delights will also be yours. A reflection of the happiness you provide to others will be returned upon you. And when, by the expansiveness of your generosity, that happiness is spread over the earth, how intense this realization is as it converges upon you from every quarter! Your enjoyment will be a participation of the highest delight of the Savior as in His great work of compassion He sees the labor of His own soul and is satisfied. May we so live that no small share of this enjoyment shall be the portion of us all!

Do not worry about how measurable or comparatively fruitful your life is. Your job is to abide, trust, yield, rest, obey, be, wait and know that the Lord of the Harvest, the Great Husbandman, and our Captain and King will use you, and fulfill His purpose in and through you (Psalm 138:8). As Hannah Whitall Smith says, "Our job is to trust, it is God's job to do."

May the Lord be pleased to draw you into a oneness with Him that you have not yet known. May you come to know the fullness of the completed work of Jesus Christ in power and faith beyond anything yet experienced. And may the Holy Spirit continually guide you into all truth, control you in every way, and generate the fruit God desires in both the quantity and quality of His choosing.

And if He places the desire in your heart to be His missionary in any way whatsoever, simply respond "yes," and await His unfolding of your future as He Himself leads you day by day, moment by moment, and brings you into the execution of His plans and His desires. "Wait for the Lord; be strong and take heart and wait for the Lord" (Psalm 27:14).

Additional Resources

1. Operation World: The Definitive Prayer Guide to Every Nation
   a. **www.operationworld.org**

2. 30 Days of Prayer for the Muslim World
   a. **www.30daysprayer.com**

3. Voice of the Martyrs
   a. **www.persecution.com**

4. Perspectives on the World Christian Movement
   a. **www.perspectives.org**

Printed in Great Britain
by Amazon

40673233R00141